2nd Edition

Student Workbook

Show What You Know®

On Ohio's Sixth Grade Proficiency Test

6th

The Leading Publisher of

Test Preparation Material for Ohio's Sixth Grade Proficiency Test

Name: _____

Englefield & Arnold Publishing

Written By: Jolie S. Brams, Ph.D.
Patricia Nay, M.A.
Joan Schrader, M.S.Ed.
Deborah Tong

Published by:
Englefield and Arnold Publishing
P.O. Box 341348
Columbus, OH 43234-1348
614-764-1211

Printed in the United States of America
05 04 03 02 01   20 19 18 17 16 15 14 13 12 11 10 9 8 7 6 5

ISBN: 1-884183-05-0

Acknowledgements ·

About the Authors:

Jolie S. Brams, Ph. D., is a clinical child and family psychologist with 20 years of professional experience. She received her doctoral degree in clinical psychology at Michigan State University in 1981. In addition to her private practice, she is an adjunct professor at The Ohio State University. Dr. Brams has evaluated and treated thousands of children, many with educational difficulties. She has appeared on national television shows, including the *Today Show*, and has lectured to Ohio schools and community groups. Dr. Brams is the contributing author of three chapters in this book: Test-Taking Strategies, Motivation, and Test Anxiety.

Patricia L. Nay, M.A., is a fourth grade teacher at Hatton Elementary School in Akron. She has worked in the Akron Public Schools for 28 years, 14 years as a Spanish teacher and 14 years as an elementary teacher. She received her bachelor's degree in Spanish and her master's degree in Elementary Administration from the University of Akron. A member of the Akron Education Association, Pat was honored as "Teacher of the Year" at Smith Elementary School. Pat has previously authored proficiency test preparation chapters and flash cards for Englefield & Arnold Publishing for the fourth and sixth grades. She is the contributing author for the Science and Citizenship chapters of this book.

Joan Schrader, M.S., has been an educator for more than 25 years. She is currently teaching American History to eighth graders at Riedinger Middle School for Akron Public Schools. She holds a Bachelor of Science degree in Elementary Education from the University of Akron and a Master of Science degree in Curriculum and Instruction from Kent State University. She has gained a reputation among teachers for mathematics presentations at district, regional, and state levels. Mrs. Schrader is the recipient of numerous awards for innovative and creative teaching. She is the contributing author for the Mathematics chapter of this book.

Deborah Tong has worked for the past eight years as an independent writer and editor. A former English teacher in New Jersey, she also worked in the Education Department of the Worcester Historical Museum in Massachusetts. A graduate of Middlebury College in Vermont, Deborah is the recipient of an Educational Press Award, the IABC Bronze Quill Award, and the Baesman Gold Medal. She is a veteran proficiency test preparation author, having written Reading and Writing chapters and flashcards for Englefield and Arnold Publishing for the fourth, sixth, ninth, and twelfth grades. She is the contributing author of the Reading and Writing chapters of this book.

Englefield and Arnold Publishing acknowledges the following for their efforts in making this proficiency material available for Ohio students, parents, and teachers:

Cindi Englefield Arnold, President
Eloise M. Sasala, Managing Editor
Mercedes Baltzell, Associate Editor
Bethany Hansgen, Project Editor
Jennifer King, Illustrator
Scott Stuckey, Proofreader

Chapter Reviewers:

Jo Hutchison
Erica Todarello Klingerman
Kathleen A. O'Dwyer
Carol Preidis

Table of Contents

Test-Taking Strategies

What are Test-Taking Strategies?

Everyone has used strategies in their lives. A strategy is a special technique that helps us when we are faced with challenges. Sometimes we figure out strategies on our own, but sometimes we learn them from the experiences and the knowledge of others. Think about a baseball coach or a dance instructor. We perform better, such as improving our batting averages or winning dance contests, because of the guidance and special hints from our coaches. A little league baseball player can be strong and athletic, but he may not perform his best until the coach gives him new ideas to help him be the best he can be.

The strategies you will learn in this book are simple strategies. Many students have found these strategies to be very helpful when facing all sorts of tests. These skills are not hard to learn, and there really aren't very many of them, but once you feel comfortable using them, you will be amazed how much better you do! The most important thing to remember about strategies is that they are not hard, but you must pay attention to these strategies and remember to use them when taking tests.

It is helpful to remember that strategies are only one part of doing well on all tests, including the Ohio Sixth Grade Proficiency Test. It is also important to practice and learn not to be nervous or anxious. Recently, a newspaper article told the story of a major league pitcher who was having no trouble throwing the ball to the batter but was having a terrible time throwing the ball to first base. This was a serious problem. Many runners were "stealing" second base because the pitcher could not throw accurately to his first baseman. The throws were wild, and one even ended up in the stands! The pitcher had never faced this type of situation and turned to his coach for help. The coach had him practice planting his left foot firmly in the dirt before throwing the ball to first base. This strategy was very effective. It seemed like a little thing at first. The pitcher knew you had to have control of the ball before you threw it anywhere, especially to first base, but he never realized he had to pay special attention to his left foot. Once he realized this, he threw accurate throws to first base, and very few runners stole bases on him after that.

Remember the baseball pitcher! There are three things about him that helped him be successful.

1. He practiced for years to master his pitching and to learn the game of baseball.

2. All his coaches, from elementary school all the way through his professional career, helped him learn strategies so he could be more successful in his pitching and baseball playing.

3. He learned to deal with nervousness and anxiety, and he became confident of his abilities. (See the chapter "Test Anxiety" to help you feel calmer about tests.)

In this book, you will find help with practicing test questions, using strategies, and learning how to feel less anxious. There are also chapters in this book that will help you review the materials you need to do well on the Ohio Sixth Grade Proficiency Test.

Let's look carefully at what types of test-taking strategies can be most helpful to you!

1. **Don't depend on luck!** People who depend on luck do not take responsibility for themselves. Some people who believe in luck do not want to take the time and effort to do well on a job or an assignment. It is easier to say, "It wasn't my fault that I didn't do well. It's just not my lucky day." Other people trust everything to luck. They feel trying is a waste of time. They feel they could never do well, no matter how hard they try. They get in the habit of saying, "Whatever happens, happens." Studies have shown that students who feel they have no control over what happens to them because they believe everything is based on luck or fate, usually have poor grades and feel poorly about themselves.

   There is a lot you can do to prepare for the Ohio Sixth Grade Proficiency Test. It is important that you do not think, "Whatever happens, happens," or believe whether you pass or fail is just luck. Instead, you need to prepare for this test by concentrating, every day, on what you can do to be as successful as you can. Keep in mind that how well you do on this test depends on you, not on luck. Read some more about luck in the following box.

Luck Isn't Enough

Have you ever had a lucky number, lucky color, or even a rabbit's foot? A famous NFL quarterback never wears new shoes if he has won a game when wearing one particular pair. It doesn't really make sense (new shoes might be better for gripping the turf and staying on his feet), but he thinks it helps. However, if he only believed in luck, he wouldn't be an NFL player. He also had to learn and practice a lot! Learning in your classroom and practicing what you learn is probably the best strategy you can have. Don't be like Chuck!

There was a cool boy named Chuck
Who thought taking tests was just luck.
He never prepared.
He said, "I'm not scared."
When his test score appears,
he should duck!

2. **Be an active learner**! In order to learn, you have to "do!" No one can learn anything by just sitting like a "couch potato." This does not mean you have to be running and jumping around while you are learning, but it does mean your mind has to be active. Students who are active learners pay attention to what is being said. They also constantly ask themselves questions about the subject. When able, they participate by making comments and joining discussions. Learning with an active mind is important in two ways. One, students who are active learners are much more successful in school. Two, students who are active learners are rarely bored. Their minds are constantly thinking about what is being taught and challenging the information they hear. The more they think about things, the more they learn, and the less bored they feel. Active learners enjoy school, learn a lot, and feel good about themselves.

How can you be an active learner? Think about a holiday dinner with a whole bunch of your relatives. Your Great Uncle Eldon is talking about his childhood. You know you have to be mannerly and stay at the table, but you wish you could leave and go to your room to play video games. Suddenly, you remember this discussion might be more fun if you could practice being an "active learner." You start looking at your Uncle Eldon and asking yourself questions about what he is saying, "I wonder how my Aunt May handled so may kids?" or "Did it ever get so cold on the farm they couldn't milk the cows?" You then learn to listen intently to find out those answers. You ask your Uncle Eldon questions that are interesting to you. You will find Uncle Eldon is not as boring as you think. You might learn a lot about history and about your family's past.

Think about the information in the next box to make you an even better active learner!

Be an Active Learner

Being an active learner means paying attention to what is being said, thinking of questions, and participating in discussions about what is being taught. Learning to be an active learner takes practice and time. If you are the type of student who is easily bored or easily frustrated, it will take some time to practice looking at the speaker and really giving some thought to what is being shared. You may want to remember to ask yourself, "Am I looking at the speaker? Am I paying attention? Do I have any questions or ideas about what the speaker is saying?" After a while, you will find active learning becomes a habit that makes you a much more successful student.

There was a young girl named Kristen
Who was bored but wouldn't listen.
She didn't train
To use her smart brain,
And never knew what she was missing!

3. **Do your best everyday!** Successful people did not become successful overnight. Instead, they made accomplishments step-by-step and day-by-day. When you think about the Ohio Sixth Grade Proficiency Test, you might feel it is too much to handle. You know you have to pass many sections, such as Writing, Reading, Citizenship, Mathematics, and Science. For many students, it seems too much to think about all at once. The best way to prepare for the test is by doing your best every day. Set goals for yourself, and try to accomplish these goals. These goals could be challenging yourself to read a book chapter every day, finishing homework, learning five new math facts, or completing practice questions at the end of your science chapter. You will be amazed at how much you learn by making an effort to do your best one day at a time. Think about the example in the next box and compare it to your own life.

Do Your Best Everyday

How many days are there in a year? You probably answered pretty quickly: 365. Imagine how much you would know if you learned just one extra fact every day of the year. At the end of the year, you would know 365 new facts. You could use these to surprise and impress your friends and family! Now, think about what would happen if you learned three new facts every day. At the end of the year, you would have learned 1,095 new facts. Soon, you will be on your way to having a mind like an encyclopedia.

Most successful people have used this strategy throughout their lives; they made a promise to themselves to do their best in school, in business, or in their professions.

There was a computer programmer who was working very hard to support his family and thought he had no extra time to start his dream of creating an Internet business. However, he didn't give up. He promised himself every morning he would do two things everyday that would help him start his business. After doing this for two years, he was on his way to meeting his dreams. He was able to develop his own business of selling all types of gifts online.

There was a smart boy named Ray
Who learned something new every day.
He was pretty impressed
With what his mind could possess.
His excellent scores were his pay!

4. **Speeding through the test doesn't help.** The Ohio Sixth Grade Proficiency Test was developed to help schools understand how much students know. Students will have two and one-half hours to finish each proficiency test. There will always be some students who finish the test more quickly than others. There might even be some students who do not have time to finish some questions. Whether you finish at a faster rate, or at a slower rate, than other students in your class is not important. As long as you take your time, concentrate well, and do your best, you should be able to show what you know. You will not get a better score if you finish the test before everyone else. Speeding through a test item doesn't help you find the correct answer. Read the following information to help you better understand why speeding is not a good test-taking strategy.

Speeding Through the Test Doesn't Help

In our world, speed seems important. We always hear about the "fastest computers," the "fastest running backs," and the "world's fastest bullet train." Speed gets people's attention and respect, but how fast you complete the Ohio Sixth Grade Proficiency Test does not affect your test score. The people who created the test did not want students to rush; they allowed two and one-half hours to finish each subject. They want you to show what you know, not show how fast you can answer questions. Speeding will not help you use any of the strategies discussed in this chapter. Look what happened to Liz.

There was a sixth grader named Liz
Who sped through her tests like a WHIZ.
She thought she should race
At a very fast pace,
But it caused her to mess up her quiz.

5. **Read directions carefully.** By the time students are in the sixth grade, they probably think they have heard every direction ever invented. They have read and listened to directions through six years of school already! It is easy to learn to "tune out" directions. Whenever we hear something over and over, it is natural to stop listening. Unfortunately, this usually causes trouble!

Think about your typical day at home. Your mother or father calls down from the top of the stairs and says, "Don't forget to let the dog back in the house!" You have had your dog since you were about five years old, and you have heard your parents say, about a billion times, that you have to let the dog in. Your mind has learned to let what your parents tell you "go in one ear and out the other." Then, when you do not let the dog back in the house, your parents become upset with you and might even punish you. Tuning out your parents only makes things worse.

It becomes easy to "tune out" directions in school, but this is not helpful. Every paper and test has different directions. If students aren't listening, they may misunderstand assignments or fail tests, not because they do not understand the material or because they aren't smart, but because they "tuned out" and did not listen to directions.

Some students do not read directions because they think to themselves, "I don't like being told what to do." When students see directions as aggravating, they cannot perform in school to the best of their abilities, or show the world what they know. As hard as it seems sometimes, listening to directions, whether from parents or teachers, helps us learn and grow so we can be confident students, happy family members, and, one day, successful adults. Students might be surprised to learn that adults actually have to follow more rules every day than students. The following information will also help you understand why it is important to read directions carefully.

Read Directions Carefully

Sometimes, we make up our minds about things before we explore and study them. Sometimes, we feel nervous or rushed and don't read or listen carefully. Sometimes, we have problems with tests because we do not read and remember directions. We think we know what will be asked, or we rush through the directions. Both of these approaches get in the way of us being able to show what we know!

Imagine you are a famous chef. You are really well known for your cakes; you make the best cakes in Ohio! One day, a visiting king and queen from a foreign country come to Ohio for a very important visit. You are asked to bake their favorite cake, one you have never baked before. They give you a list of ingredients and directions. However, you barely look at the directions. "Who has time? I know how to bake any cake without any directions." Unfortunately, you don't read that the cake needs to bake at 250°, not the 350° temperature at which you usually bake your cakes. You also don't read that it should only bake for 15 minutes. Your recipes call for cakes to be baked for 30 minutes. What do you get? Crispy cake and upset royalty. Not a good combination!

Read Directions Carefully

Reading directions slowly, repeating them to yourself, and asking yourself if they make sense are powerful test-taking strategies.

There was a nice boy named Fred
Who forgot almost all that he read.
The directions were easy,
But he said, "I don't need these!"
He should have read them instead.

6. **Don't get stuck on one question.** It is normal to worry or panic when you are in a situation in which you do not know the answer. When people panic, they generally "get stuck." Getting stuck doesn't happen on tests alone. Think about mountain climbing or rock climbing. There probably isn't a more dangerous sport. You have to have a tremendous amount of muscular strength and also a lot of courage to climb up cliffs, even if you are attached to safety ropes. Climbers seem to get into the most trouble when they feel "stuck." Sometimes they will come to ledges or cliffs and not know where to go next. They "freeze" and have no idea where to next place their hands or feet. Sometimes climbers have to be rescued by having fellow climbers check out their positions and give them instructions on where to go next. While hanging on, they might think all sorts of negative thoughts such as, "I have no idea what I am doing," or "I'll never be good enough at this," or "I know I'm going to fail." Their feelings are very similar to the types of feelings students have when they feel "stuck" on test questions.

Everyone will find that certain test questions are difficult on the Ohio Sixth Grade Proficiency Test. So, if you are stuck, you are not alone! The road to success is finding strategies that will help you become "unstuck." The best advice is to remember that not knowing one question does not mean you will fail the Ohio Sixth Grade Proficiency Test. There are many test questions, so there is room for you to show what you know. Think to yourself, "This is just one question out of many," or "I don't have to have a perfect score to pass."

Going on to other questions may actually help you remember what you thought you couldn't remember before! Remind yourself there is nothing wrong with circling a question number you aren't sure about and coming back to the question later. This is an excellent test-taking strategy. Look at the next box to think about getting "unstuck."

Don't Get Stuck on One Question

You can lower your chances of "getting stuck" on the Ohio Sixth Grade Proficiency Test if you practice "getting unstuck" at different times while at school and at home. Most successful people think in ways that are "flexible." Flexible thinking is just a fancy term for learning to think about ideas in many different ways and learning to move on when you are stuck. Flexible thinking helps us remain cool and calm and also helps us come up with new ideas and answers when we didn't think any existed.

Think about how you might feel if you were invited to a friend's swimming party on a Saturday afternoon. You have been looking forward to this party for weeks. Suddenly, on Saturday morning, your mom tells you, "I'm really sorry Misty, but I have to go to work all day today because we are having a crisis at the office. I don't think I'm going to be able to take you to the party." Your first reaction would be feeling terribly "stuck" and probably angry and sad, all at the same time. However, if you could "take a step back" from the problem you are facing, you might be able to find a solution.

For example, you might go along with your mother to work. Maybe she works fairly close to your friend's house, and maybe one of the other moms at the party can come and pick you up. You might also ask your mom if she could drop you off at your friend's house early in the morning. Maybe you could call up your friend's mom and ask her if you could be of some help in setting up the party. You also might ask neighbors to give you a ride to the party, and in exchange, you would walk their dog or maybe babysit for a few hours. When you let yourself get "unstuck," you will find there are often solutions to even the hardest problems.

Use the strategies in this chapter, and also look at the chapter titled "Test Anxiety." Both of these chapters have ideas that will help you become "unstuck" and learn to be a "flexible thinker." Think about Von!

There was a sweet girl named Von
Who got stuck and just couldn't go on.
She'd sit there and stare,
But the answer wasn't there.
Before she knew it, all the time was gone.

7. **Power guessing is a helpful strategy.** Very rarely do we have the exact answers for everything. Some facts we might "know by heart." For example, if someone asks us, "What is $100 \div 10$?" We immediately know the answer is "10." We really don't have to worry about guessing because it is a fairly simple question. However, most of us guess all the time in our day-to-day lives, and we really don't even know we are doing it.

Let's say you are shopping for a "thank-you" present for a neighbor who helped you fix your bike. Your neighbor is a very nice 65-year-old man. You have never asked him what he wants for a present, because your gift is supposed to be a surprise. So, how do you know what to get him? You figure it out by "power guessing." Think about what you know about your neighbor. For a start, your neighbor likes gardening. You also see him outside all the time in blue jeans and a t-shirt. When it is cold, he wears a denim jacket that matches his blue jeans. Now you have another clue: your neighbor likes to wear denim. When you go shopping, you are better prepared to make a good guess. Look for things in the store that have to do with gardening. Keep a close look out for gifts that might be made of denim. All of a sudden, you spy a denim bag that hangs in the garage and holds all sorts of small garden tools. What a perfect gift! You have used your power guessing to come up with a really good answer.

On the Ohio Sixth Grade Proficiency Test, power guessing means using all you know to sort out answers that may be possibly right or possibly wrong. For example, you are asked, "How many streams are there in Ohio?" You are given the possible choices of 57, 100, 700 or 3300. You have a great deal of information to use to guess at the right answer, even if you don't know the exact answer. Think of a map of Ohio. You know there are more than 57 streams in Ohio. There are possibly even more than 100 streams; some streams are not as big as the Ohio River and are rather small. Certainly, Ohio could have more than 100 streams if most of them were small. Think of how many bridges, built over streams, you have driven or walked over. Therefore, you have decided 57 and 100 could not possibly be correct. This leaves two answers that might be right. You have already increased your chances of getting the question right by 50%. This is a pretty good strategy! There is even more to know about power guessing. Think about the following information. The answer is 3300.

Power Guessing is a Helpful Strategy

Did you know that on the Ohio Sixth Grade Proficiency Test there is no penalty for guessing? Some of us have learned guessing is "bad" and thinking is "good." Actually, guessing and thinking can go together with great results! It's okay to guess, and its even better when you learn how to guess intelligently. Think about Tess!

There was a smart girl named Tess
Who thought it was useless to guess.
If a question was tough,
She just gave up.
This only added to her stress.

Test-Taking Strategies for Different Types of Questions

Multiple Choice Items

There is a lot to learn about how to do your best and show what you know on multiple choice questions on the Ohio Sixth Grade Proficiency Test. The good news is, these test-taking strategies are easy to learn, and they get results. The other piece of good news is, there is always one right answer out of the four choices offered. The multiple choice questions on the proficiency tests do not have "none of the above" or "all of the above" as possible answer choices. The test is designed so you can use all your test-taking strategies and all that you have learned in school to do the best job possible.

When you take the test, don't forget all the test-taking strategies you have read about in this chapter:

- don't count on luck
- don't speed through your test
- be an active learner
- study your best every day to prepare
- read directions carefully
- don't let yourself get stuck on one question
- always use power guessing

These strategies are helpful in all your test-taking experiences. The following are some strategies that might help you when you are faced with multiple choice questions.

1. **Because every multiple choice question is different, it is very important to read the question and <u>all</u> four answer choices carefully.**
    You have already learned how important it is to read directions carefully. Now, think about the simple (but disastrous) mistakes that you can make if you do not read answers carefully! Not reading answers carefully can have the same bad result as not listening carefully in class or other situations. Imagine yourself at a large amusement park. There are rides everywhere, big and small, all sorts of game booths, concession stands, movie theaters, lights, and sounds everywhere. It is quite a confusing place! You are there with your scout troop, and everyone is deciding where the group will meet in an hour. Your scout leader says, "We can either meet at the Double Coaster, the Water Park, the Double Dipper, or the Wet and Wild." You are excited about being at the amusement park. All the answers sound about the same to you. What you remember is "Wet and Wild," but you didn't listen carefully enough. Everyone has decided to meet at the "Water Park" instead. You wait for an hour at the "Wet and Wild," but your scout troop is nowhere to be seen. They eventually find you, and it ruins pretty much the whole afternoon. You should have listened carefully to all the possible choices!

    Paying attention to details in the question and in the answer can help you use all you know to make the correct choice. Let's practice with the following example.

    Mr. and Mrs. Jamison own a travel agency that specializes in selling vacations to sunny Florida and the Caribbean Islands. They want to increase their business by selling more vacations to people who live in Ohio. What would be the best way to accomplish this goal?

A. Advertise in Florida newspapers that they have inexpensive and exciting trips for sale.

B. Write letters to the editor in the Columbus, Cleveland, and Cincinnati newspapers complaining of our snowy weather and gray skies.

C. Raise their prices so people will think their vacations are the best.

D. Share interesting information about their travel agency and vacations with people who read *Ohio Magazine*.

If you looked at these answers quickly, you might be tempted to choose Choice A. Choice A is partially correct. It would be a good idea to advertise in newspapers because many people would see the information. However, advertising in Florida newspapers is not helpful. People in Florida already live with sunny skies and no snow. No one in Ohio would see the Florida newspapers. If you read Choice A too quickly, you would miss the word "Florida" and get the answer wrong. Choice B does not directly tell people to go to Florida or to the Caribbean. It makes them feel bad about the weather in Ohio, but it does not give them ideas about what to do to make their vacations more enjoyable. Choice C does not make sense because of what we know about capitalism. We know that higher prices do not encourage people to buy. Thus, Choice D is correct. Sharing interesting information about Florida and the Caribbean in an Ohio magazine will draw the attention of Ohio readers. They might want to give Mr. and Mrs. Jamison a call about vacations.

2. **The test-scoring computer is not as smart as your brain, so give it all the help you can!**
Most sixth graders have had the opportunity to take tests that require them to fill in a "bubble" with a #2 pencil in order to mark the correct answer. It is very important to mark the correct answer on the Ohio Sixth Grade Proficiency Test. Even if you know the correct answer on multiple choice questions, the computer will not be able to score your correct answer if you do not completely fill in the answer "bubble" so it is dark. Computers may be smart, but they do not equal the human brain. Computers will not look at your answer sheet and say, "Well, the pencil line is kind of light, but I know that Tyler meant to fill in answer C." The computer will incorrectly read, "Tyler didn't answer anything for question 13." This is not what you want to happen!

You also want to be very careful to make sure you fill in the correct answer bubble for each question. Don't get confused and fill in the incorrect bubbles. Take your time, and look carefully at the answer sheet.

Practice correctly filling in bubbles on an answer sheet.

○   ○   ○   ○   ○   ○   ○   ○   ○   ○

3. **Don't always pick the first answer that seems right.**
   Although some of the choices on the Ohio Sixth Grade Proficiency Test may be absolutely incorrect, other answers may be partially correct or may relate to just one small part of the question that is being asked. It is important not to answer with the first choice that seems even partly "on target." It is well worth the time to read every answer choice and consider each one as carefully as possible. You always need to think about the question because multiple choice answers may have correct statements in them that are not directly related to the question being asked. Think about the following example:

   Encyclopedias have been around for many years. In the 1920s, when libraries were scarce and American citizens wanted their children to become more educated, people saved up money for years in order to buy encyclopedias their children could use at home to help them do better in school. Encyclopedia salespeople would go door to door selling encyclopedias to families. This was a big business back then. Encyclopedias were huge books, and an entire set of encyclopedias might take up 25 volumes. This was more than what would fit on three or four bookshelves in the average family home!

   Now it is much easier to find the information contained in encyclopedias. Many encyclopedias are online, and students can use them free of charge. Libraries are also much more common today. They are also generally closer to people's homes, and because of cars and public transportation, students have more opportunities to get to a library. There is also a lot of information from other sources that used to only be available in encyclopedias. Students can gather information from the Internet, through newspapers and magazines, and through educational television. In the year 2000, fewer and fewer people buy encyclopedias for their homes, although some people buy encyclopedias on CD-ROMs for their computers. Students now learn how to gather information from many different sources in order to learn about the world around them.

   What is the major idea discussed in this selection?

   A. There isn't much work left these days for encyclopedia salespeople.

   B. In the year 2000, there is information available from many sources.

   C. Education for children has been an important part of our American heritage.

   D. Encyclopedias, in book form, take up a lot more room than encyclopedias on CD.

Choice A is not entirely incorrect; there certainly is less work today for encyclopedia salespeople than there was in the 1920s. However, this is not the main point of the passage. There was a discussion about encyclopedia salespeople to explain why encyclopedias have been important over time, but that is just one detail of a much bigger idea. Choice C is also partially correct. If you picked out this answer as your first guess, you would have been only partially correct. It is true the United States has become a strong country because of education, but it is not the main point of the passage. The same holds true for Choice D. We know CD-ROMs take up less room than books, but this is not the main point. Choice B is correct. The purpose of this passage is to explain that in the year 2000, information is much more varied and much more widely available than the encyclopedias of years ago.

4. Use what you know to "power guess!"
Earlier in this chapter there was a discussion about power guessing. When you power guess, you use what you know about a subject, along with your common sense, to come up with the best answer possible. Let's look at the following example to see how power guessing works.

Much of Ohio's water supply comes from rivers and man-made lakes and dams. Ohio's citizens and visitors use these bodies of water for recreation, such as fishing, boating, swimming, and jet skiing. What is the most important thing we can do to reduce pollution in the water without ruining everyone's fun?

A. Add chlorine to the water to make it safer to drink.

B. Install plenty of trash cans at beaches, campgrounds, and boat docks so people will not throw garbage in the water.

C. Only allow power boats and jet skis to use kerosene instead of gasoline to power their motors.

D. Have park rangers conduct annual inspections of boats and jet skis to make sure they are not leaking fuel and their engines are running effectively.

Choice A talks about adding chlorine to water. If you have gone swimming in a swimming pool, you are familiar with chlorine. You also may have heard chlorine is added to drinking water to make it safe to drink. It would be very difficult to add chlorine to large bodies of water because truckloads of chlorine would be needed to have any effect. In addition, chlorine would kill fish and animals. Chlorine will not rid the water of pollutants such as industrial poisons. Using your common sense and your ability to power guess, Choice A is probably not correct. Think about Choice B. While you know it is disgusting to think about people throwing garbage in the water, you know it probably happens. It is unlikely, though, that installing trash cans is the best prevention against pollution. How many times have you seen garbage on the ground around a trash can? Choice B is not the best answer. Next, think about Choice C. You know kerosene is a fuel and so is gasoline. Both of these are burned, therefore, causing pollution. Kerosene doesn't seem much better than gasoline, and you remember from history lessons that early settlers used kerosene for lamps. It burned with a nasty and polluted smell. It doesn't seem to make sense to use kerosene to power boats. If you did, it would probably cause more pollution. Thus, Choice D is correct. It is the job of park rangers to protect the safety of Ohioans and visitors in our natural areas. It would probably make sense for them to make sure all boats and jet skis pollute the water as little as possible.

5. Use your pencil to "attack" the test!
Your pencil can be helpful in finding the correct answer. This test-taking strategy helps you to organize your thinking while you are taking the test. Developing a "system" of crossing out wrong answers and circling important information helps you focus on the question and think more clearly. Good test takers do not just use their "brains" but also their "eyes" to help them figure out the correct answers. Also remember that circling the numbers of questions that made you feel "stuck" helps when you go back and try to answer those questions again. Let's try using a pencil to make sense of the following question.

Map makers will probably never be out of a job because maps are constantly changing. What changes listed below would not cause a map maker to make changes in a map of the United States?

A. erosion

B. changes in population

C. election of a new president

D. the completion of an interstate highway

First, you must look carefully at the question. Remember, this question wants to know what would "not cause a map maker to make changes" on a map. This tells you there are more answers that would cause a map to be changed. Using your pencil, you might want to circle the word "changes." You also might want to circle the word "not." As you go through the answers, you may want to circle or cross out certain answers that seem right or wrong. Some students might find it easier to cross out wrong answers, while other students may find it easier to circle what they feel are correct answers. You and your teacher can find out which strategies are best for you when using your pencil to find the correct answer on multiple choice questions. Soon, you see Choice C is correct. A new president doesn't cause a map to change. However, erosion of beaches, new highways, and growing cities do cause changes on a map.

Short-Answer Items

Short-answer questions are very different than multiple choice questions. For multiple choice questions, you are given four possible answers. You use different thinking skills to figure out the correct answer. This chapter taught you many strategies that can be used with multiple choice questions, such as power guessing and being careful not to choose the first answer that seems correct. Short-answer questions are more challenging for some students. Short-answer questions require students to respond with ideas and conclusions of their own. Coming up with new ideas is different than picking out correct answers. Remember, you will be asked short-answer questions for Reading, Citizenship, Science, and Mathematics. It is important to carefully read the following and practice writing short-answer questions. Practice leads to success. When you practice, you should use strategies to help you do the best you can.

1. **Read the question carefully.**
   The first thing you need to do when asked a short-answer question is make sure you clearly understand what the question asks. It is impossible to come up with a correct answer if you do not understand the question. When computers were first invented, computer scientists coined the phrase "garbage in means garbage out." What they meant was, computers cannot be "smart" unless you give them the right information. If you give computers the wrong instructions, no matter how fancy or expensive your computer may be, the answer will always be wrong. If you do not know what is being asked on the Ohio Sixth Grade Proficiency Test, then all you can respond with is an incorrect answer. You may be a very smart student and very motivated to do well on the Ohio Sixth Grade Proficiency Test, but just like the computer, you need to remember that what goes in wrong will definitely come out wrong.

2. **Question yourself like a detective.**
   Once you have correctly read the question, you have to act like a detective and "search your mind" to find the right answer. Detectives are always asking themselves questions. When detectives come upon crime scenes, they do not believe the first answer or conclusion that comes to their minds. For example, suppose a detective comes to a crime scene, and there is a fingerprint in the hallway. The detective does not say, "This fingerprint most likely belongs to the thief." Instead, the detective asks many questions. In fact, the fingerprint could be from another police officer who touched a wall in the hallway! The detective never stops asking questions. You need to do the same when asked short-answer questions.

Think about the short-answer question and ask yourself if what you are thinking about makes sense. Some students actually say the questions to themselves, as if they were talking, and then they say the answers. They make believe they are having conversations. If the conversations do not make sense, they go back and see how they could respond more clearly.

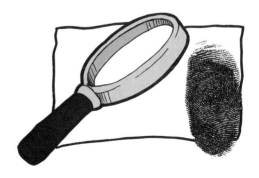

Think about being asked a short-answer question about something you know well. You really aren't listening closely, and the answer you give does not make much sense. For example, most students know the name of their principal. Suppose you were in the front hallway of the school, and a visitor asked you for the name of the principal. You are only half listening and answer, "It's down the hallway past the water fountain." You thought you were asked where the principal's office is located, but the visitor really needed the name of the principal. If you had repeated the question and your answer to yourself, you would have realized the two together did not make sense.

As you think through the question, remember the role of being a detective. Keep asking yourself whether the answer you are giving makes sense and goes along with the question that is being asked.

3. **Use your pencil wisely.**
   You can use your pencil to your benefit when asked short-answer questions. There is no penalty for writing in the margins of your test booklet. Writing down ideas, even if they turn out to be the wrong ideas, is still helpful. It lets you "see" what you are thinking about and helps you to remember key points, especially during a stressful test situation. Writing down ideas is always smart. Remember, some of the most successful people keep a note pad with them at all times and quickly write down ideas that come to their minds.

   A recent television show about rock musicians revealed many famous recording artists always keep pencils and pads of paper with them. They write down parts of song lyrics and even little ideas that grow into large ones. Sometimes they write down ideas for the music itself. You can also use your pencil to write on any charts, graphs, or maps included in your test. Be careful not to write all over the diagram so you do not understand what you are seeing. For example, if a map asks you to identify important geographical landmarks that make a difference in people's lives, you may want to circle the important landmarks on the map. In your short-answer, you can discuss them one at a time, remembering not to leave anything out.

4. **Write as neatly as you can, and think about how your answer will fit in the space provided.**
   Many people joke, the messier your handwriting, the smarter you may be! They point out that many doctors have really bad handwriting. This may be a joke, but drug stores and pharmacies are very worried about this problem. If the pharmacist cannot read a doctor's handwriting, a patient may get the wrong medication. This can be a very serious situation. Your handwriting is also an important part of doing well on the Ohio Sixth Grade Proficiency Test. You will not be given a bad mark because your handwriting is not neat, but if your handwriting cannot be read, it will create problems for scorers. On this test, you may write either in cursive (script), or you may print. Even if you have always disliked having to take the time to write neatly, it is impor-

tant to make an extra effort to do your best Ohio Sixth Grade Proficiency Test so other people can see how much you know. You do not have to use all the space given in your test booklet, but some students find their writing can be neater if they use all the space provided.

Before writing your answer, it is important to look at the answer space to estimate whether what you have to say will fit in the space provided. This is another reason why practice is so important. Practicing writing answers to short-answer questions will give you a better idea of how to put your ideas down on paper in an organized and understandable fashion. Writing is important for all the proficiency tests.

5. **Always remember to review your work.**
   Always review what you have written. This is a good strategy for all your schoolwork, but it is especially important in doing well on the Ohio Sixth Grade Proficiency Test. Reread the question, and then read your answer. Again, you need to think like a detective and ask yourself, "Does my answer make sense?" You can always correct what you have written or perhaps come back to the question at another time.

Extended-Response Items

Extended-response questions ask you to respond in a more complex or lengthy way than short-answer questions. Usually, you will be asked to provide more detailed explanations or descriptions that relate to the question being asked. Extended-response answers are longer than short-answer responses and require your writing to be more organized. Many of the test-taking strategies you will use for responding to short-answer questions can be used when you are faced with an extended-response question.

1. **Remember, extended-response questions usually require a detailed answer in which you have to support your conclusion.**
   Detailed responses are important in doing well on extended-response questions. For example, suppose a science, short-answer item asked, "List two reasons why hibernation is necessary for certain mammals." You could list your response with either full sentences or partial sentences. You would be graded on whether you understood the importance of hibernation. An extended response item might be, "Discuss why global warming would hurt the growth of forests." In

this instance, you are asked to discuss an idea. This means using longer sentences and giving many details to support your conclusion.

2. **Organize your thoughts by using your pencil to write in the margins of the test booklet.**
   Using your pencil to organize your ideas for short-answer questions is always a good idea, but it is really important when you are asked an extended-response question. It is perfectly fine, and usually helpful, to write sentences or even parts of sentences in the margins of your test booklet. Some students find it helpful to write the beginning of each paragraph in their margins. Then, they can organize how their final product will appear. Suppose you were asked, "What are the problems Himalayan climbers encountered when they ran out of oxygen?" You might want to scribble, in the margins of your test booklet, your ideas for your first through fourth paragraphs. You could write in the margins of your test booklet:

   1. High altitude sickness . . .
   2. Feeling confused and losing direction . . .
   3. Feeling physically sick . . .
   4. Being exposed to cold . . .

Now you can complete each idea by writing brief paragraphs in your answer booklet

Test Anxiety

What is "Anxiety?"

By the time you are in the sixth grade, you probably have said the word "nervous" more times than you can remember. Think back to all the times you have said, "That really made me nervous," or "If that happens, everyone's going to be really nervous!" Most of us think we have a pretty good idea about what it feels like to be nervous, and most of us would not want to be nervous if we had a choice. What most people don't know is that we can all learn to control our nervous feelings.

The definition of the word "nervous" is similar to the definition of "anxiety." Sometimes, instead of saying, "I feel nervous," people say, "I feel anxious." Both words, "nervous" and "anxious," are words most people would describe as "bad feelings." Sometimes the word "anxious" can be used in happier terms, such as when someone says, "I'm really anxious about being old enough to be a camp counselor." When people use the word "anxious" in this way, it usually means they are looking forward to something new or exciting, but they still feel a bit uncomfortable or worried about what might happen. It may be fun to be a camp counselor, but most sixth graders would worry about things that might happen when they are given such responsibilities. They may even wonder whether they can handle the job. Even though we might look forward to new experiences, there is some degree of worry and concern that makes us feel a little uncomfortable.

When Do We Become Anxious?

If we want to stop uncomfortable feelings, we need to remember times we felt poorly. When we understand situations that make us feel anxious, we are one step closer to fighting those uncomfortable feelings and being more in control of our lives. Once we know it is normal to feel a certain way, we have a better chance of changing how we feel. People may feel anxious during any of the following situations.

People feel nervous or anxious when they see or observe something scary or frightening. One example would be watching a horror movie. Watching slimy snakes jump out of darkness, or hearing howling sounds in the middle of the night, would make anyone feel anxious. What we see in the movie makes us feel uncomfortable. During a scary movie we may say, "That creepy music makes me feel really nervous!"

Our life experiences can also make us feel anxious. Going on a roller coaster for the first time (or even for the hundredth time) causes most people to experience some uncomfortable feelings. Ask almost anyone how they felt as the roller coaster was ever so slowly chugging and clanking its way to the top of the hill. Most people would say, "I felt pretty nervous!"

Our thoughts can make us feel anxious. Surprisingly, scientists have found thoughts are actually more powerful than observations or experiences in making people feel nervous or anxious. It is important to remember thoughts are powerful in making you feel both good and bad. There are only so many things we see or do that make us feel nervous, but there are probably hundreds and hundreds of thoughts that can make us feel uncomfortable and anxious. Our minds are very creative when thinking about what could happen. Scientists have found people who often feel anxious have many powerful negative thoughts controlling their lives. They are always thinking about what will happen in the future or what will make them nervous. During a typical school day, students' minds might be filled with thoughts about being called on in class, not being able to sit with a certain group of friends, embarrassing themselves on the basketball court, or wearing the wrong clothes. The more you think negative thoughts, the more anxious you get! The best way to feel more confident is by controlling your negative thoughts.

What Does It Feel Like To Be Anxious?

Feeling anxious makes us feel physically uncomfortable and also makes us behave in ways that are not helpful to the current situation.

Anxiety causes unpleasant changes in our bodies. When we are anxious, we feel our hearts racing, feel sick to our stomachs, and feel we can hardly catch our breaths. Feelings of anxiety can appear as though they are real physical illnesses, and in fact, many people who are anxious go from doctor to doctor wondering what is wrong with them. They do not realize their problems come from being anxious or nervous. The physical feelings we experience with anxiety can be strong and scary.

Anxiety also causes changes in our behaviors. When feeling anxious, most people will do anything to try to feel better. Many people try to get rid of anxious feelings using methods that are not helpful. They may try to avoid what makes them anxious; they may become confused about how to relieve their anxiety and do nothing at all; or they might become so upset that they actually make themselves more anxious.

Think about taking your first airplane ride, alone. You are in the sixth grade and certainly smart enough to figure out how to behave on an airplane. You know to read the airport signs telling you where to go, but your brain is telling you this is a new experience that could possibly be dangerous. There may be a problem with the plane. Your grandmother might forget to meet you when the plane lands. What if someone talks to you on the airplane, and you feel too shy and don't know what to say? Your anxiety might cause you to behave in ways that are not helpful to the situation. You may beg your parents to put off the trip until a later time, you may cry and become upset, or you might even try to walk away from the airport gate.

The Negative Cycle of Anxiety

Anxiety causes negative thoughts. The more anxious we become, the more negatively we think. Our negative thinking makes us feel more anxious. When one thing leads to another, then another, then another, and the whole situation gets increasingly worse. This is called a "negative cycle." One of the big problems with feeling anxious is finding one's self in a negative cycle. In this negative cycle, anxious thoughts cause uncomfortable physical feelings. Those uncomfortable physical feelings and negative thoughts cause us to change our behavior in ways that make us feel the problem will never get better. When we feel the problem will never get better, we get more anxious and act in ways that do not help the situation. When the situation is not helped, we have more bad feelings and thoughts. See the problem? The anxiety goes on and on, and generally gets worse. However, if you can understand how your thoughts, physical feelings, and behaviors all work together to create problems, then you can understand how to fix those problems.

What Can We Do About Being Anxious?

There is great deal that can be done to stop our anxious feelings and make us more confident in ourselves. You would be surprised to learn how many famous and successful people have been anxious in their lives but learned to overcome their problems. They didn't start out successful or famous, but they did start with a great deal of anxiety. If they can find ways to solve their anxiety problems, you can too!

The Story of the Nervous Rap Musician

Most sixth graders look at popular musical performers and think to themselves, "Those guys have it all together!" Most popular musicians look as if nothing can bother them. They dance around stage, acting as if they are on top of the world. They never seem afraid of making mistakes; they never look as though they're worried about anything. Most sixth graders would probably be surprised to know many musicians have fears and anxieties they have had to learn to control.

There is a well-known rap musician who has an interesting life story to tell. Throughout his life, he has had to fight strong feelings of anxiety in order to share his music with the world. This rap star was born into a musical family. Almost everyone sang, danced, or played a musical instrument. He had an uncle who was a famous jazz musician, and his sister was a movie star. As this young man was growing up, his mother encouraged him to sing in church. He was a good singer, but he felt very shy. He always worried about making a mistake; he was afraid people would laugh at him. He was concerned people would think he had less talent than other members of his family. He always felt anxious, but when he was young, he depended on his mother to help him think positively and practice his music. He felt somewhat calmer singing in church when his mother sat in the audience. When he was eleven, his cousins offered him the chance to train to become a rap musician. They felt that because he had an excellent voice and a good sense of rhythm, he would probably be successful. Everyone thought this was a wonderful opportunity for him to enjoy music, express himself, and maybe one day be famous. Unfortunately, this young man's anxiety got in his way. He could not stop thinking negative thoughts that made him more and more nervous. All day long, he would compare himself to the best rap musicians. He doubted his talent and ability to compete with successful artists. His heart would race, and he felt sick to his stomach whenever he looked at his audience. He did not see his mother or other familiar faces from his church. Instead, he saw all sorts of strangers whooping and hollering, all wanting more music. He knew this was a good reaction, but it made him nervous.

This young man wanted to be a rap artist, so he had to find some way to solve his anxiety problems. With the help of his family and friends, he realized when he wore a hat pulled way down over his eyes, he didn't have to look at the audience. This helped him with his anxiety; it also made him look rather cute! He became known for his floppy hat and his cool appearance. He also learned to try to block out thoughts that made him nervous. Whenever he thought, "I'll never be that good," or "I'm bound to make a mistake," he took a deep breath and forced himself to stop thinking those thoughts. Instead, he would say, "I have a lot of talent," or "If I make one little   mistake, it won't matter," or "Because everyone in my family is a good musician, I have a great chance of being a success, too." He learned to change his negative thoughts into positive thoughts. Eventually, he became a rap artist who shared many positives ideas with his audience. Through his songs, he taught others to think positively about their world and to solve problems. His music made his own life happy, and he helped change the lives of other people. He was able to do all this because he overcame his own anxious feelings.

You Can Do It Too!

To be successful, this rap star did many things to help himself with anxiety. You can do these things too! Let's look carefully at what he did, as well as some extra things you can do, to be successful.

Understand and accept yourself! People who are most anxious are those who are most hard on themselves. They think there is something terribly wrong with them, believing they are the only ones in the world who are anxious. This is definitely not true! In fact, more than 80% of sixth graders report they feel anxious at least once a day. Think about that! This means eight out of every ten sixth graders have at least one anxious feeling during a typical day. In sixth grade, everyone is trying to be grown-up and independent. This makes sixth graders less likely to tell others when they feel anxious or unsure. However, most of your classmates are feeling the same way, even if they don't admit it. You may feel anxious, but more than likely, you are not the only one.

Try to figure out what causes your anxious feelings. Anxiety is not something you catch, the way you may catch a cold. Anxiety is something you feel or experience. Usually, when you catch a cold, you have a pretty good idea why you are coughing and sneezing. Maybe your little brother or sister was sick and made you sick. Maybe everyone at school is under the weather, and it becomes obvious you came in contact with the cold germs at school. This is a fairly easy mystery to solve. Things get harder when thinking about the sources of anxiety. For most of us, anxiety comes from overreacting to past experiences. When something bad happens to us, we usually have physical feelings as well as negative thoughts that go along with the experience.

Imagine a hot summer day at the pool. You are having a wonderful time. You and all your friends are splashing in the pool, playing water games, eating junk food, and generally having a great time. You have climbed up the stairs to the diving board and jumped off many times on this sunny and fun day. All of a sudden, when you are climbing up the diving board stairs, your wet feet cause you to slip. You don't fall because you grab onto the hand rails, but you get scared. Your heart races. You know you could have fallen to the concrete and bruised yourself, if not worse. You carefully climb down the stairs and go and sit on your towel with your friends. You look at the diving board as if it is the scariest thing in the world. At that point, you made an "anxious connection" between feeling afraid and the diving board. You were especially anxious about climbing up the stairs. Your slip was something really big that happened. You almost fell climbing the stairs of the diving board, although you had done it successfully many times before. Now the experience is different. Your body and mind are all racing together. You come to the conclusion, "Don't ever do that again!"

Generalization. Remember the cycle of negativity? While sitting on your towel, the cycle begins. You start thinking to yourself, "I'm not as coordinated as my friends," or "I always make a fool of myself." Then you start thinking about all the other stupid things you could do or might do. As time goes on, not just that day but days later, you keep thinking about other things that make you nervous or afraid. Your fears increase over time. This is called "**generalization**." It means you transfer a frightening feeling from one situation to another. Soon you become afraid to do more and more things.

For many students, a similar situation happens with tests. There probably isn't anybody in school who has not done poorly on at least one test. Most likely, almost everyone has been given a challenge they didn't think they could meet. Even the smartest students in school have been challenged by tests that have been difficult or tests for which they were not prepared. However, when students are very anxious about tests or school, even in very early grades, they can begin to get a sense that tests in school make them anxious. From that point on, their thoughts and feelings enter a negative cycle, and they are afraid to take tests.

When you think about the causes of your test anxiety, think about the past. Was there ever a time (a particular grade or a particular subject) that made you feel very anxious? Did you ever find yourself feeling more anxious after that point in time? You owe it to yourself to think about your past and consider whether there was a situation that made you feel anxious. Did you generalize your thoughts and feelings from that situation? If you did, you might now feel that tests are scary, and that you are unable to do well in a test situation. However, what you are thinking and feeling may not be true!

Historians and archeologists all look to the past to understand the present. They are detectives trying to connect past experiences to recent events. Think about yourself as a detective investigating your own past. Have your past experiences made you anxious when facing tests in the sixth grade?

Understanding yourself and your history will make you a more confident person in many ways. Many of us do not pay attention to all the positive things we have done. We don't realize we have overcome stress and anxiety in the past. Some middle school students find it interesting to sit down with their parents or other family members and find out what they were like when they were younger. What challenges did they face? How did they deal with those challenges? Have they overcome an obstacle that seemed impossible?

Momento Exercise

A momento is something that reminds you of the past, like your grandmother's charm bracelet or a souvenir from a vacation. The Momento Exercise is a helpful exercise you can complete if you want to review your past. Ask family members for photographs and other things that show your successes over the years. For example, looking at your baseball trophies from first grade will bring back memories of what it was like to play baseball for the first time. You may recall how you overcame your worries about not learning basic skills and playing on a team. Looking at your second grade report card and seeing how you improved your grade in math from a "C" to a "B" says you have been successful in difficult situations. You used skills to help you with your problems. If you are feeling test anxiety (or if you just want to feel really good about yourself), try the Momento Exercise.

Momento Exercise

Gather five photographs, certificates, or other remembrances from your past. Lay them out on a table and ask a parent or adult who knows you to tell you a story about each item. What were you doing in the photo? How did you earn the certificate? Then, write down what you have learned about your abilities from those stories. An example is shown below.

Item	What happened	What I learned about myself
Model car	I built it without my Dad's help.	I can be successful on my own.

Dealing With Your Physical Reactions To Anxiety

Anxiety feels bad. When people feel anxious, their bodies react in ways that cause them discomfort. People who experience anxiety may feel flutterings in their stomachs, their hearts may race, and they also might feel as if the world is spinning around them. Anxiety causes these physical problems because anxious thoughts and stressful experiences cause changes in the brain and body. Although these feelings are uncomfortable, you can easily feel better using some simple exercises that help put your brain and body back in control.

Change The Way You Breathe To Feel Calmer!

Changing the way you breathe can make your feelings of anxiety lessen or even disappear. Controlling your breathing slows your heartbeat and helps you focus and feel more in control. Try to control your breathing and anxiety by taking deep breaths and letting them out slowly. Fill your lungs with air. While your lungs are full, count to five silently. Slowly let go of that breath. You should do this very slowly, counting silently to five as you exhale. If you do this ten times or so, you will find that by focusing on your breathing, you're changing the way your body functions. This results in feeling less anxious and more in control.

Relax Your Muscles!

Find a quiet place where you will not be interrupted by other people or be distracted by noises. Make yourself as comfortable as possible. Sit up straight with your feet on the floor and your hands, with palms up, in your lap. After finding a comfortable position, close your eyes. You are ready to begin relaxing your muscles.

Make your muscles as tense as you can while you count to four. Hold your tense muscles to the count of four and then relax them to the count of four. Begin with the muscles in your feet. Tighten these muscles and count, "one . . . two . . . three . . . four." Then relax your muscles while counting to four. How does the relaxation feel? Remember the feeling so you will know what you are striving for in the future. You should start to feel relaxed in the areas you tightened. Repeat the process of tightening to a count of four and relaxing to a count of four on all your major muscles. You should work on your lower legs, your thighs, your buttocks, your stomach, your chest, your arms, your hands, and even your face. Finish by scrunching your forehead, much like a person who is thinking, and then letting it go.

While you are tensing your muscles, make sure you breathe deeply and slowly. It is always best to breathe deeply while tensing and relaxing your muscles at the same time.

If you are short on time, space, or concentration, just do one or the other. You can do deep breathing exercises, or you can tense and relax your muscles. Either way, you are doing something to help yourself be a positive person and a good test-taker.

Think About Being Calm!

Use visualization to reduce anxiety. **Visualization** is just a fancy word for filling your mind with positive thoughts and images so anxiety does not take over your thinking. There are two types of visualization. One type of visualization is letting your mind think about pleasant experiences, such as going to the beach, playing with your friends, listening to music, skateboarding, going shopping, or any type of pleasant activity you enjoy. The second type of visualization is to see the opposite of what makes you afraid. If you are scared of taking a test, you need to visualize success. There is some truth to the idea that if you expect to fail, and you think about failure over and over in your head, you increase the chances of making that failure come true. But, if you expect to succeed, you increase your chances of success. Practice, in your mind, what it will be like when you do well on the test. Picture yourself turning in the test and walking proudly and happily out of the room. Be creative in thinking about your test-taking as a success and not as a failure.

The best part of breathing, relaxing, and visualization exercises is noticing a change in your thoughts about yourself. The exercises help you believe, "By doing some simple things, I can overcome this anxiety." When you think back to the negative cycle, you will find that if you can stop your negative thoughts or your bad, physical feelings, the cycle will be broken. By relaxing your body physically and your mind mentally, you will start to break the negative cycle of anxiety.

Learning to Recognize Negative and Incorrect Thoughts

Our thoughts are powerful. Thoughts can cause anxiety, but they can also help us get rid of anxiety. Your thinking can prevent test anxiety. At the very least, your thoughts can make it much easier for you to calm down and take tests.

Thoughts that make us anxious are either negative thoughts or incorrect thoughts or beliefs. **Negative thoughts** cause us to look at the bad side of things. Negative thoughts usually focus on one little, bad part of a whole picture, which might not really be all that awful. Imagine you are traveling to the beach for the weekend with your family, including your seven-year-old sister and four-year old-brother. You know you are going to have to help your mom look after them. As most sixth graders know, it is not so easy traveling with two younger siblings. You might love your little brother and sister, but they can get on your nerves! You can choose to look at the situation negatively, allowing yourself to become very upset, stressed, and anxious. You can tell yourself, "The drive to the beach will be awful. They won't leave me alone, and they will bug me to death. I will hate this whole weekend. I wish I could stay home." In this example, you are making a very big deal out of one small problem with the vacation.

Another way to look at the situation would be to tell yourself, "Well, it might be aggravating having them on the car ride to the beach, but I will bring my CD player. Maybe I can bring some card games, and we all can play games so they will be quiet and behave. I can read my new mystery book while they take a nap. My mom will also play with them, and I will have some private time to myself. I might even meet some other kids my age." In the second example, you recognize your vacation may not be perfect, but you have thought about positive parts of the situation. You have thought about solutions for dealing with your little brother and sister.

Incorrect beliefs are beliefs that may not be negative, but may make you feel poorly about a situation. Many sixth graders facing proficiency tests, or other tests, think and believe no one else has the same problems. They feel very much alone and tell themselves, "I am the only person who can't handle my problems." They believe everyone else has their lives under better control. They feel there is something wrong with them. These are incorrect thoughts. The truth is, sixth grade can be a fun year, but it is also a difficult year for most students. It is a time of change and growth, and any type of change is not easy. You are not alone in worrying about how well you do in school or whether you are as smart or as successful as your friends and other students.

What Types of Negative and Incorrect Thoughts Seem Real To You?

Many sixth graders have many of the same thoughts and feelings with regard to tests. Here are some examples to show the types of feelings middle school students have when they worry about tests.

Stay-Away Stephanie

Stephanie's first thought when faced with a test in elementary school was to avoid the situation. She felt so anxious, she did almost anything to avoid facing a test situation. Stephanie tried many things to avoid taking tests. She begged her guidance counselor to keep her out of these situations. She told her parents she was too sick to go to school. One time, Stephanie purposely stayed in the school library, rather than going to class. She knew she would receive a detention and a stern lecture from the principal, but she would do anything to avoid a test. Stephanie found the ways she handled her problems in elementary school did not work in middle school. She realized she couldn't run away from her problems. Instead of finding ways to overcome her anxieties, she had focused on them. This just made it worse! She was caught in the cycle of negative thoughts, and Stephanie could not seem to escape.

Worried Wendy

Wendy was the type of sixth grader who always looked for the worst thing to happen. She had many negative thoughts. Even in situations that may have resulted in good things, Wendy always focused on the bad things. She exaggerated everything bad and forgot about everything good. She found her mind racing a mile a minute with all sorts of thoughts and ideas as to what would happen when she failed a test. She found herself believing her teachers would see her as a failure if she performed poorly. She thought her friends would think she was stupid. She believed her parents would be terribly angry. She forgot her friends liked her for reasons other than her grades, her parents thought she was wonderful, and her teachers saw her as a nice kid and a hard worker. No one was going to hold it against her if she performed poorly on a test. Wendy would be very surprised to hear that she might be very successful. Her negative thoughts get in the way of anything positive.

Critical Chuck

Chuck was the type of sixth grader who spent all his time putting himself down. No matter what happened, he always felt he had been a failure. He was never able to look at his past history and understand he had had many successes in his life. Even when he did look back, he thought about the negative, not the positive. Chuck did not have a good sense of who he was or from where he came. He would have had much less test anxiety if he was able to appreciate all the successes he had had when he was younger. He should have been proud of all his positive qualities. But, because he didn't appreciate or understand himself, Chuck had test anxiety.

Victim Vince

Most sixth graders find that it is important to take responsibility for their actions. It helps them understand adulthood is just around the corner, and they are smarter and more able than they ever thought. Vince was not like this. He couldn't take responsibility for himself. He thought everything was someone else's fault. He did not feel comfortable acting like a mature sixth grader who wanted to take responsibility for his actions. All he did was complain about others and especially about tests. He told himself and everyone else, "They made that test too hard. The teachers were all unfair. Besides, I never could study at home because my parents let my little brother make too much noise. There was nothing I could do about my problems; it was everyone else's fault." Vince ended up with test anxiety. He thought nothing he did would help, and he didn't want to change his ways. He felt the world was against him. His attitude made him feel hopeless, sad, worried, and unable to do well on tests.

Perfect Pat

Everyone knows in sixth grade there is more homework and responsibility. Everyone in sixth grade needs to try his or her best, but no one should try as much as Pat. All Pat did was worry. She felt no matter what she did, it was never good enough. She wrote book reports over and over, and she studied for tests until she was exhausted. Trying hard is fine, but Pat worked so much, she never felt she had done enough. Because she never accomplished what she set out to do, she worried all the time and felt anxious. This anxiety got in the way of her doing well on tests and made her life unhappy.

Change Negative Ideas into Positive Ideas

Negative thoughts are strong thoughts, but positive thoughts are even more powerful. Positive thoughts are thoughts you create to gain control over your life. Anything you create is always better because it's yours! You have a responsibility to be a detective and find out whether a negative thought is really correct, especially when tests are involved. You have to convince yourself that some of your ideas may not be correct or helpful, even when they seem very real. Ask yourself questions to find out if your negative thoughts are true. Answer the questions below about negative thoughts you have had regarding tests and other difficult situations.

1. What is a negative thought I have about tests?
   Example: My mind goes blank when I am worried.

   _____

   _____

2. What evidence is there that my negative thoughts about tests are true?
   Example: Once or twice, I have been nervous while asking pop quizzes.

   _____

   _____

3. What evidence is there that my negative thoughts about tests are not true?
   Example: I did well on my Scout citizenship test with no problem!

   _____

   _____

4. If I believe my negative thoughts, what could happen?
   Example: I could tense up and not trust my abilities.

   _____

   _____

5. If I believe my positive thoughts, what could happen?
   Example: I could be calm and successful.

   _____

   _____

The way we talk to ourselves has to do with how we think and feel, as well as what we accomplish. How we talk to ourselves is just as important, if not more so, than how others talk to us.

Think about Troy who is car salesperson. Troy knows how to talk to a customer so the customer will buy what he is selling. Salespeople are trained to make positive statements and to look at the positive side of a situation. Think about going to the car dealership with your family to try to buy a car. Your father says to Troy, "I don't think we want this van with leather seats. Leather is too expensive." Troy doesn't say, "You're right, it's really a bad idea to buy a van with leather seats." Instead he says, "Well, leather seats might be a little more expensive, but they will last longer and save you money in cleaning." Troy changes a negative idea into a positive idea because he wants to sell the car. Below, there are three ways to make positive statements work for you.

1. **Use the "I" word.** Focusing on what you can do, instead of what other people do, makes you feel much more in control and positive about yourself. Instead of stating, "Everyone is going to do better than me on the math test," state, "I will do well on the math test." It is better to think about what you can do rather than comparing yourself to others. The salesperson says, "I can sell a lot of cars this week," not, "Everyone else will sell more cars."

   In the space below, write down some "I" statements that put you in control!

   _____

   _____

   _____

   _____

2. **Avoid using the word "not."** Say to yourself, "I will be calm during the test," instead of, "I will not be nervous during the test." When the word "not" is included in a sentence, one usually has put a bad thought in the sentence. Think back to Troy. Suppose the car your father is buying is a nice car but not a very expensive car. Because he is a smart salesperson, he will say to your father, "This is an inexpensive car and a good deal for the price." He will not say, "This is not an expensive car," because that will make your father feel he is buying a cheap car. If your father feels that way, he may not buy any car at all!

   In the space below, write some positive sentences. Do not include the word "not." It would be very helpful to write these positive sentences about test-taking.

   _____

   _____

   _____

   _____

3. Think about the opposite of your negative idea. If math is your poor subject, state, "I think clearly about many things, so I can give math a good shot." Think again about Troy the salesperson. If he thinks, "I'll never sell a car to this guy. He's too cheap," that negative thought will cause him to have anxiety and stop him from being the best salesperson he can be. Instead, Troy should replace his negative thought with a positive thought and state, "This man does not want to spend a lot of money, but I bet I can find him an inexpensive car he will like." Troy will probably be successful in selling your father a less expensive car.

In the space below, write some negative ideas and change them into positive ones.

_____

_____

_____

_____

Test Anxiety Scale

Students who have anxiety about the Ohio Sixth Grade Proficiency Test may have anxiety when thinking about other tests as well. On the next pages, take the following true/false test to see how anxious you are when thinking about tests and test-taking.

Test Anxiety Scale

How much test anxiety do you have? Circle either "true" or "false" for the following questions.

1. While taking an important test, I am afraid I am not as smart as others.   true   false

2. If I were to take a test measuring how smart I am, I would worry a great deal before taking it.   true   false

3. If I knew I was going to take a test measuring how smart I am, I would not feel confident and relaxed.   true   false

4. While taking an important test, I sweat a lot.   true   false

5. During tests, I think of things that don't have anything to do with the test.   true   false

6. I feel very nervous when I have to take a pop quiz.   true   false

7. During a test, I think of what will happen if I fail.   true   false

8. Before, during, or after important tests, I am often so tense my stomach gets upset.   true   false

9. I freeze up on quizzes, tests, and exams.   true   false

10. Getting good grades on one test doesn't seem to make me more confident on the second.   true   false

11. I sometimes feel my heart beating very fast during important tests.   true   false

12. After taking a test, I always feel I could have done better than I did.   true   false

13. I usually get depressed, sad, or upset after taking a test.   true   false

14. I have an uneasy, upset feeling before taking an exam.   true   false

15. If there is a test coming up, I act angry and tough about it.   true   false

16. During a test, I often wonder what I know.   true   false

17. I seem to defeat myself while working on important tests.   true   false

18. The harder I work at taking a test or studying for one, the more confused I get.   true   false

19. As soon as an exam is over, I try to stop worrying about it, but I just can't.   true   false

20. During exams, I sometimes wonder if I'll ever get through school.   true   false

21. I would rather write a paper than take a test.   true   false

22. I wish tests did not bother me so much.   true   false

23. I think I could do much better on tests if I could take them alone and not feel pressured by time limits.   true   false

24. Thinking about the grade I may get in a class bothers my studying ability and performance on tests.   true   false

25. If tests could be done away with, I think I would actually learn more.   true   false

26. If I don't know a test answer right away, I get nervous.   true   false

27. I really don't see why some people don't get upset about tests.   true   false

28. Thoughts of doing poorly interfere with how I do on tests.   true   false

29. I would rather do lots of extra homework than take a test.   true   false

30. Even when I'm well prepared for a test, I feel very anxious about it.   true   false

31. I don't enjoy eating before an important test.   true   false

32. Before an important exam, I find my hands or arms trembling.   true   false

33. I feel the need to "cram" before an exam.   true   false

Count the total number of "true" answers. This is your test anxiety score. If your score is below 8, your anxiety is pretty low. If your score is between 8 and 20, it is in the medium range. Students in this range would probably benefit from reading this book carefully and trying to change some of their test-taking behaviors. If you score above 20, you probably have high test anxiety and need to ask your teacher or guidance counselor for special help. Remember, just because your score is high does not mean you will fail tests or you cannot learn to feel less anxious. It just lets you know you should look for some help so you can be the best student possible and show what you know.

Is Anxiety Ever Helpful?

Throughout this chapter, you have learned anxiety is generally not a good thing. It interferes with your ability to do as well as you can on tests. It also affects other areas of your life. However, you might be surprised to learn some anxiety, but not too much, might actually be helpful.

Some Anxiety is OK, but Too Little or Too Much isn't Helpful!

Everyone knows "couch potatoes" are rarely successful people. They have no energy and no worries about anything. Basically, they have no anxiety. They live their lives like "bumps on a log." Without some degree of anxiety, nothing ever gets done. They fail tests because they don't worry at all! Problems also arise when someone has too much anxiety and worry. People's uncomfortable physical feelings, their racing thoughts, and their desire to escape gets in the way of their success.

When professional sports teams are going to play an important game the next day, coaches know how to make their players anxious enough to do well, but not so anxious the players can't play. The night before the game, coaches usually have team meetings, and they give "pep talks." In the pep talks, they tell their players about their strengths and talents, and they let the players know they can be successful. Coaches also try to make players a little worried and anxious by reviewing the strengths of the opposing team. Then, to calm the team down, they usually go out for dinner or a movie. Coaches try to get their teams to be anxious and concerned but not to be overly negative. If coaches tell their teams, "Don't worry, you'll do fine, you're the greatest athletes ever," the teams won't focus on their jobs. If the coaches tell the teams, "You're the worst people ever, and you're never going to do well," the result will also be negative.

Another example about the positive effect of having some anxiety could be related to ketchup and french fries. For most kids, eating french fries with no ketchup is boring. When one starts to put ketchup on fries they become tastier and tastier, up to a point. However, with too much ketchup the fries are soggy and taste mainly like ketchup, not crisp and delicious fries. They quickly become less tasty and, in fact, eventually become quite disgusting.

DIAGRAM I

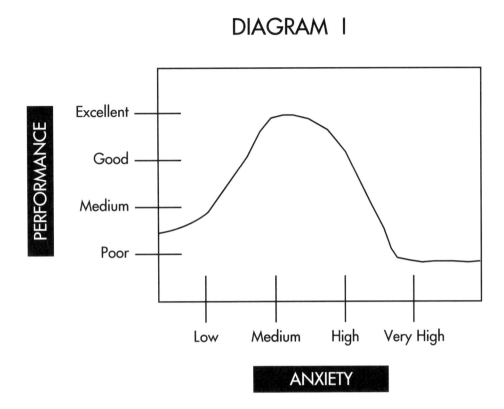

The same can be said for anxiety. You will find an "anxiety curve" in Diagram I. This graph shows the relationship between the amount of anxiety a person can have and how well they will do. You might want to use this chart when thinking about your performance on tests. If you have too little anxiety, you probably will not perform well, but once you reach a certain point and have too much anxiety, your performance rapidly becomes worse. The lesson to be learned is that prior to tests, such as Ohio Proficiency Tests, it is important to feel a little concerned but not overly worried.

This information will help you not only on tests but in other areas of your life. On the next pate, take a minute to complete the chart titled "How much anxiety is helpful?" to better understand the relationship between anxiety and how well you perform in different situations. The first example is about asking someone you don't know very well to your birthday party. If you do not have anxiety, you probably will not get a positive response. If you have too much anxiety, you also will probably not get the results you desire. It is best to have a "medium level" of anxiety to get the right results.

Fill in the chart titled "How much anxiety is helpful?" Explain how a sixth grader might feel in the following situations. The first one is done for you.

How much anxiety is helpful?			
Type of Challenge	No Anxiety	Medium Anxiety	High Anxiety
1. Asking someone you don't know very well to your birthday party.	I really don't care if the person I invite doesn't want to attend my party.	I feel a little shy about asking this person to my party.	I feel sick to my stomach. I'm going to ask a friend to give the invitation.
2. Giving a speech at the sixth grade awards dinner.			
3. Taking an airplane ride alone, across the county, to see your grandmother.			
4. Performing in front of your classmates at the school talent show.			

Writing

Practice Writing I

Directions: Read the following passage or follow along as the passage is read aloud to you.

Take me out to the ball game,
Take me out to the park.
Buy me a hot dog and a Coke.
I don't care if we all go broke!

So it's root, root, root for the home team.
If they don't win, it's a shame,
For it's costing us $28 bucks apiece
To see a pro ball game.

Use the ideas in this poem to complete three writing activities.

First activity: Write a letter to the owners of your favorite professional team. In this letter, explain why you think professional sporting events should be more affordable for families. Offer some ideas to help the owners make tickets less expensive.

Second activity: You will write a personal essay. In your essay, discuss some family activities that are fun and inexpensive.

Third activity: You will write an invitation to an elderly neighbor inviting him or her to attend a non-professional or a minor league sporting event with you. In your invitation, offer reasons that will make your neighbor want to attend the event.

The pre-writing activities will give you ideas for your letter, your personal essay, and your invitation. The pre-writing will not be scored. You are not allowed to use a dictionary or a thesaurus in your pre-writing. Spell words to the best of your ability.

Pre-writing 1

Directions: The questions below will give you ideas for your letter to the owners of your favorite professional team. Write your ideas on the lines provided.

What is the name of your favorite professional team?

_____

_____

Why should professional sporting events be more affordable for families?

_____

_____

_____

How much do you think it should cost to go to a professional sporting event? (Include the cost of the tickets, parking, food, and beverages.)

_____

_____

List several ideas to help team owners lower the costs of tickets and concessions (food).

_____

_____

_____

Look at your cost-reducing ideas. How will each idea help make tickets less expensive?

_____

_____

_____

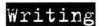

Pre-writing 2

Directions: The headings in the web below and the box on the next page will give you ideas for your personal essay about inexpensive family activities. Write your ideas in the web and in the spaces provided in the box. Example ideas are provided.

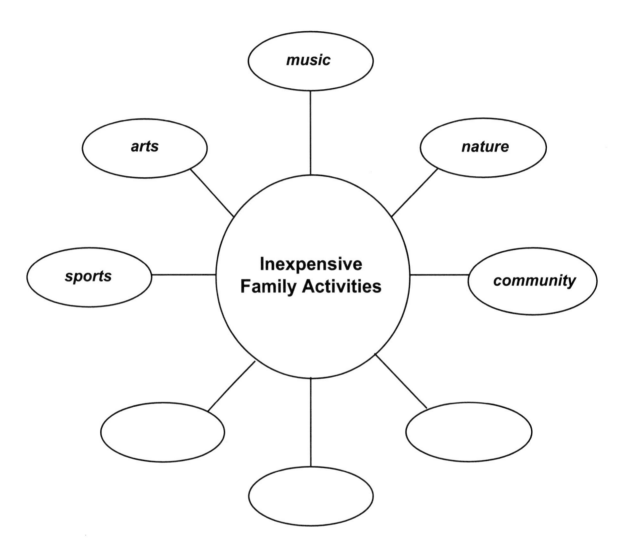

Write your ideas here.

Favorite family activities	Why we enjoy this activity	Approximate cost per person
biking on the local bike trail	*it's outdoors on a pretty trail*	*Free! We have bikes and helmets.*

Pre-writing 3

Directions: The headings below will give you ideas for your invitation to an elderly neighbor. Write your ideas on the lines provided.

What kind of non-professional or minor league sporting event will you attend?

_____

_____

Why would your neighbor be interested in going with you?

_____

_____

What are some title ideas for your invitation? For example, "See a Big Game in a Small City!"

_____

_____

What are the details of your invitation (date, time, etc.)?

_____

_____

Go on to the next page to begin Exercise 1A.

Exercise 1A: Persuasive Letter

Directions: For Exercise 1A, you will write a persuasive letter to the owners of your favorite professional team. In your letter, explain why you think professional sporting events should be more affordable for families. Offer several ideas to help the owners make tickets less expensive. You may use the ideas you wrote in the first pre-writing activity. Tell why it is important for families to be able to afford to go to professional sporting events. Give several ideas for reducing the costs of tickets and concessions (food). Use words that make your meaning clear. Your letter should be well organized and in the form of a letter. Write your letter in the space provided.

The writing you do for Exercise 1A will be scored. Look at the box below. Checklist 1A shows what your writing must include to receive your best score.

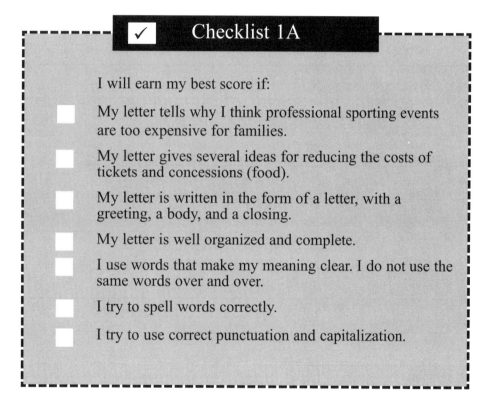

✓ **Checklist 1A**

I will earn my best score if:

☐ My letter tells why I think professional sporting events are too expensive for families.

☐ My letter gives several ideas for reducing the costs of tickets and concessions (food).

☐ My letter is written in the form of a letter, with a greeting, a body, and a closing.

☐ My letter is well organized and complete.

☐ I use words that make my meaning clear. I do not use the same words over and over.

☐ I try to spell words correctly.

☐ I try to use correct punctuation and capitalization.

Use your pencil to write your letter. You may erase, cross out, or make other editing changes to your work. You may not use a dictionary or thesaurus in your writing. Spell words to the best of your ability. Remember, writers often make changes as they work.

Exercise 1A: Persuasive Letter

_____

_____

_____

_____

_____

_____

_____

_____

_____

_____

_____

_____

_____

_____

_____

_____

_____

_____

_____

_____

_____

_____

_____

_____

_____

_____

_____

_____

_____

_____

_____

_____

_____

_____

_____

_____

_____

_____

_____

_____

_____

When you finish writing your persuasive letter, use the checklist to revise and edit your work. When you have finished checking your persuasive letter, and you are satisfied with it, you may go ahead to the second activity, Exercise 1B.

Exercise 1B: Personal Essay

Directions: For Exercise 1B, you will write a personal essay about inexpensive family activities. In your essay, discuss some family activities that are fun and inexpensive. Explain why your family enjoys these activities, and discuss how families can do many different things together without spending a lot of money. Use the information you wrote in the second pre-writing activity. Your essay may be true or not true. Your essay should be well organized and complete. Write your essay in the space provided.

The writing you do for Exercise 1B will be scored. Look at the box below. Checklist 1B shows what your writing must include to receive your best score.

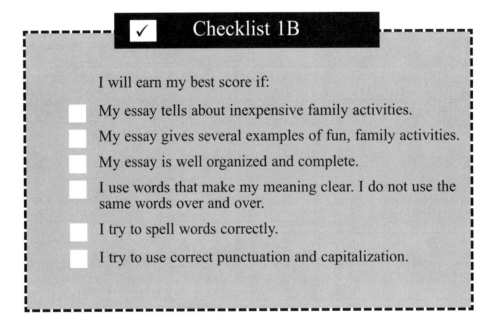

✓ **Checklist 1B**

I will earn my best score if:

☐ My essay tells about inexpensive family activities.

☐ My essay gives several examples of fun, family activities.

☐ My essay is well organized and complete.

☐ I use words that make my meaning clear. I do not use the same words over and over.

☐ I try to spell words correctly.

☐ I try to use correct punctuation and capitalization.

Use your pencil to write your essay. You may erase, cross out, or make other editing changes in your work. You may not use a dictionary or thesaurus in your writing. Spell words to the best of your ability. Remember, writers often make changes as they work.

Exercise 1B: Personal Essay

_____

_____

_____

_____

_____

_____

_____

_____

_____

_____

_____

_____

_____

_____

_____

_____

_____

_____

_____

_____

_____

_____

_____

_____

_____

_____

_____

_____

_____

_____

_____

_____

_____

_____

_____

_____

_____

_____

_____

_____

_____

_____

_____

_____

When you finish writing your personal essay, use the checklist to revise and edit your work. When you have finished checking your personal essay, and you are satisfied with it, you may go ahead to the third activity, Exercise 1C.

Exercise 1C: Invitation

Directions: For Exercise 1C, you will write an invitation to an elderly neighbor. In the invitation, invite your neighbor to a non-professional or a minor league sporting event. In your invitation, offer reasons that will make your neighbor want to attend the event. You may use the ideas you wrote in the third pre-writing activity. Explain why you want your neighbor to join you. Give specific details about the event day. Use words that make your meaning clear. Your invitation should be well organized and be in the form of an invitation or a letter. Write your invitation in the space provided.

The writing you do for Exercise 1C will be scored. Look at the box below. Checklist 1C shows what your writing must include to receive your best score.

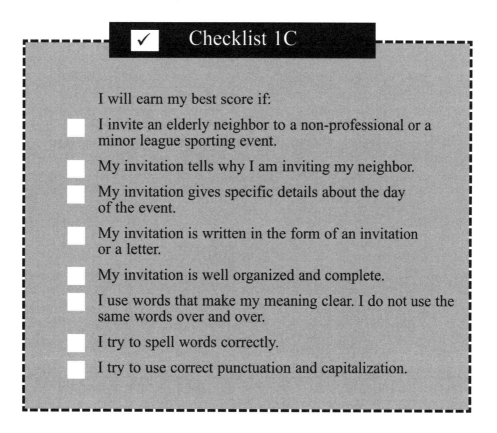

✓ Checklist 1C

I will earn my best score if:

☐ I invite an elderly neighbor to a non-professional or a minor league sporting event.

☐ My invitation tells why I am inviting my neighbor.

☐ My invitation gives specific details about the day of the event.

☐ My invitation is written in the form of an invitation or a letter.

☐ My invitation is well organized and complete.

☐ I use words that make my meaning clear. I do not use the same words over and over.

☐ I try to spell words correctly.

☐ I try to use correct punctuation and capitalization.

Use your pencil to write your invitation. You may erase, cross out, or make other editing changes in your work. You may not use a dictionary or thesaurus in your writing. Spell words to the best of your ability. Remember, writers often make changes as they work.

Exercise 1C: Invitation

_____

_____

_____

_____

_____

_____

_____

_____

_____

_____

_____

_____

_____

_____

_____

_____

_____

_____

_____

_____

_____

_____

_____

_____

_____

_____

_____

_____

_____

_____

_____

_____

_____

_____

_____

_____

_____

_____

_____

_____

_____

_____

_____

When you finish writing your invitation, use the checklist to revise and edit your work.

Practice Writing II

Directions: Read the following statement or follow along as the statement is read aloud to you.

Have you ever read the books *Hatchet* by Gary Paulsen, or *The Cay* by Theodore Taylor, or *Robinson Crusoe* by Robert Louis Stevenson? All of these books have main characters who survived being stranded for a long time in a remote location.

Use the idea of being stranded to complete three writing activities.

First activity: You will write a fictional story. You will tell a story of how someone became stranded in a remote location.

Second activity: You will write a journal entry. Imagine you are stranded. In your journal entry, describe how you have survived two days on your own.

Third activity: Write a thank-you note. In your thank-you note, thank the people who rescued you from being stranded in a remote area.

The pre-writing activities will give you ideas for your fictional story, journal entry, and thank-you note. The pre-writing will not be scored. You are not allowed to use a dictionary or a thesaurus in your pre-writing. Spell words to the best of your ability.

Pre-writing I

Directions: The lists of ideas you create below will give you ideas for your fictional story. Write your ideas in the spaces provided.

List some ideas for the personality of your main character. Two examples are done for you.

afraid of snakes _____   *independent* _____

_____   _____

_____   _____

_____   _____

Sometimes, it helps to think first about the ending of your story and work your way to the beginning. For your fictional story, list some locations where your main character might become stranded. An example is done for you.

on a mountain with no trails _____

_____

_____

_____

_____

How did your main character become stranded in this isolated location? An example is done for you.

she fell asleep at lunch and was left behind

What will your main character need to do in order to survive? An example is done for you.

she will need to look for food

Pre-writing 2

Directions: The following charts will give you ideas for your journal entry.
Write your ideas in the space provided. An example is done for you.

During the first few days of being stranded, what did you accomplish and what were your greatest challenges?

Accomplishments	Challenges
learned to make a fire	*avoiding snakes*

What is it like to be stranded? What has happened these first few days? What are your emotions? Fill in the chart below. An example is done for you.

Event	Emotions
found a wild blueberry patch	*happy, because I'm not as hungry*

Pre-writing 3

Directions: The headings below will give you ideas for your thank-you note. Write your ideas on the lines provided.

Where were you stranded? How long were you there?

_____

_____

_____

_____

Who rescued you?

_____

_____

_____

_____

What were your reactions when you knew you were going to be rescued?

_____

_____

_____

_____

Thank-you notes often mention what the writer will do with his or her gift. What will you do with your new safety and freedom?

_____

_____

_____

_____

Go on to the next page to begin Exercise 2A.

Exercise 2A: Fictional Narrative

Directions: For Exercise 2A, you will write a fictional narrative. In your narrative, explain how someone became stranded in a remote location. Include many details about how your main character became lost. Use the ideas you wrote in the first pre-writing activity. Use specific details and descriptions. Use words that make your meaning clear. Your story should be well organized. Write your story in the space provided.

The writing you do for Exercise 2A will be scored. Look at the box below. Checklist 2A shows what your writing must include to receive your best score.

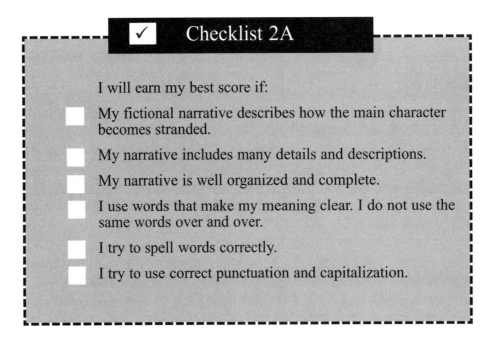

✓ Checklist 2A

I will earn my best score if:

☐ My fictional narrative describes how the main character becomes stranded.

☐ My narrative includes many details and descriptions.

☐ My narrative is well organized and complete.

☐ I use words that make my meaning clear. I do not use the same words over and over.

☐ I try to spell words correctly.

☐ I try to use correct punctuation and capitalization.

Use your pencil to write your story. You may erase, cross out, or make other editing changes in your work. You may not use a dictionary or thesaurus in your writing. Spell words to the best of your ability. Remember, writers often make changes as they work.

Exercise 2A: Fictional Narrative

_____

_____

_____

_____

_____

_____

_____

_____

_____

_____

_____

_____

_____

_____

_____

_____

_____

_____

_____

_____

_____

_____

_____

_____

_____

_____

_____

_____

_____

_____

_____

_____

_____

_____

_____

_____

_____

_____

_____

_____

When you finish writing your fictional narrative, use the checklist to revise and edit your work. When you have finished checking your narrative, and you are satisfied with it, you may go ahead to the second activity, Exercise 2B.

Exercise 2B: Journal Entry

Directions: For Exercise 2B, you will write a journal entry. You will imagine you are stranded. In your journal entry, describe how you survived two days on your own. You may use the information you wrote in the second pre-writing activity. Your journal entry should be well organized and complete. Write your journal entry in the space provided.

The writing you do for Exercise 2B will be scored. Look at the box below. Checklist 2B shows what your writing must include to receive your best score.

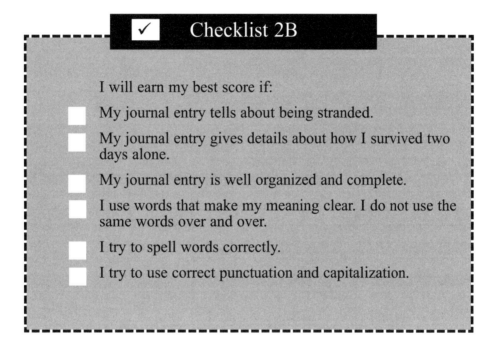

✓ **Checklist 2B**

I will earn my best score if:

☐ My journal entry tells about being stranded.

☐ My journal entry gives details about how I survived two days alone.

☐ My journal entry is well organized and complete.

☐ I use words that make my meaning clear. I do not use the same words over and over.

☐ I try to spell words correctly.

☐ I try to use correct punctuation and capitalization.

Use your pencil to write your journal entry. You may erase, cross out, or make other editing changes in your work. You may not use a dictionary or thesaurus in your writing. Spell words to the best of your ability. Remember, writers often make changes as they work.

Exercise 2B: Journal Entry

_____

_____

_____

_____

_____

_____

_____

_____

_____

_____

_____

_____

_____

_____

_____

_____

_____

_____

_____

_____

_____

_____

_____

_____

_____

_____

_____

_____

_____

_____

_____

_____

_____

_____

_____

_____

_____

_____

_____

_____

_____

_____

_____

When you finish writing your journal entry, use the checklist to revise and edit your work. When you have finished checking your journal entry, and you are satisfied with it, you may go ahead to the third activity, Exercise 2C.

Exercise 2C: Thank-You Note

Directions: For Exercise 2C, you will write a thank-you note. In your thank-you note, thank the people who rescued you from being stranded in a remote area. Use the ideas you wrote in the third pre-writing activity. Explain why you are thankful for being rescued. Use words that make your meaning clear. Your thank-you note should be well organized and in the form of a letter. Write your thank-you note in the space provided.

The writing you do for Exercise 2C will be scored. Look at the box below. Checklist 2C shows what your writing must include to receive your best score.

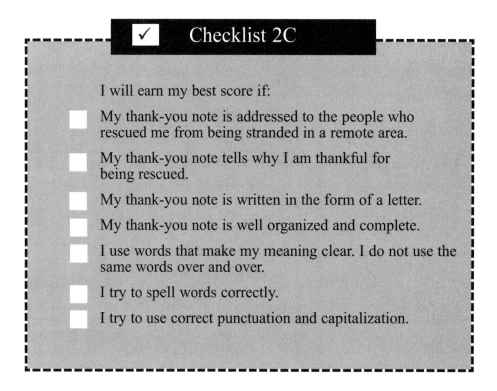

✓ Checklist 2C

I will earn my best score if:

☐ My thank-you note is addressed to the people who rescued me from being stranded in a remote area.

☐ My thank-you note tells why I am thankful for being rescued.

☐ My thank-you note is written in the form of a letter.

☐ My thank-you note is well organized and complete.

☐ I use words that make my meaning clear. I do not use the same words over and over.

☐ I try to spell words correctly.

☐ I try to use correct punctuation and capitalization.

Use your pencil to write your letter. You may erase, cross out, or make other editing changes to your work. You may not use a dictionary or thesaurus in your writing. Spell words to the best of your ability. Remember, writers often make changes as they work.

Exercise 2C: Thank-You Note

_____

_____

_____

_____

_____

_____

_____

_____

_____

_____

_____

_____

_____

_____

_____

_____

_____

_____

_____

_____

_____

_____

_____

_____

_____

_____

_____

_____

_____

_____

_____

_____

_____

_____

_____

_____

_____

_____

_____

_____

_____

_____

_____

_____

When you finish writing your thank-you note, use the checklist to revise and edit your work.

Practice Writing III

Directions: Read the following passage or follow along as the passage is read aloud to you.

Summer Day: 2100 A.D.
by Tom Williams

The whole world is under the influence of the sun. Its warming and life-giving rays beat down on the Earth. Today, the heat is at its fiercest, and not everyone is pleased by the golden light. The natural shields, that once protected us from the deadly solar rays, are mostly gone.

The sun shines down, year after year. It has not changed from last year, last century, or even last millennium. There was a time, however, when we did not worry about ozone holes and ultraviolet rays. Skin cancer was a rarity, not something guaranteed after a few hours of exposure.

The clouds have boiled away, and the sky is at its most intense shade of blue. Once, this was considered a good sign, but now we know the deeper blue the sky, the more dangerous the ultraviolet rays.

Plants that flourished during the warmth and rain of spring are battling the heat. Their leaves turn brown and wither. Animals do not move in the middle of the day; they hide in shadows or burrows.

As I wander along in the dusk, I ponder the summer of past days, when people walked during daylight without concern.

Give me back the days when a clear summer sky meant hours of fun, not a need to burrow and hide. Give me back the days when an overcast sky was a rare dampener and not a highly desired event. Then a person could experience the feeling of the warm sun on the skin and not fear the consequences.

If only I could go back in time a hundred years, then I would know summer is a time for pleasure. "Fun in the sun" would be a literal statement, not a joke. But the past is beyond my reach, and it is too late for my generation to erase the mistakes of generations past.

Use the ideas in the story to complete three writing activities.

First activity: You will imagine you live in the year 2100 A.D. Write an article for your school's summer newsletter. In your article, explain the dangers of spending the summer in the sun.

Second activity: You will write an informational essay. Again, you will pretend you live in the year 2100 A.D. In your essay, offer many tips about how to protect yourself from the dangers of the sun's rays. Give ideas of how kids can have fun without being exposed to the dangerous rays of the sun.

Third activity: You will write a set of directions. In your directions, tell how to build a park that is safe from the sun's rays.

The pre-writing activities will give you ideas for your newsletter article, your informational essay, and your set of directions. The pre-writing will not be scored. You are not allowed to use a dictionary or a thesaurus in your pre-writing. Spell words to the best of your ability.

Pre-writing 1

Directions: The questions below will help you organize ideas for your newsletter article. Write your ideas in the spaces provided.

In the year 2100 A.D., according to the story, why are the sun's rays so dangerous?

_____

_____

According to the story, what can happen to people if they spend too much time in the sun?

_____

_____

_____

_____

In the story, what happens to animals and plants in the summer?

_____

_____

_____

According to the story, why is the term "fun in the sun" a joke?

_____

_____

_____

_____

Pre-writing 2

Directions: The prompts below will give you ideas for your informational essay. Write your ideas in the space provided.

Using ideas from the story, and ideas of your own, list how kids could protect themselves from the sun.

_____

_____

_____

_____

List some activities children could do, both indoors and outdoors, that will not expose them to the sun's dangerous rays.

_____

_____

_____

_____

Pre-writing 3

Directions: Imagine you live in the year 2100 A.D. Your town built a park that is safe from the sun. Write a set of directions describing how this park was built. The headings below will give you ideas for your directions. Write your ideas on the lines provided.

Where is the park located? Why was this location chosen?

_____

_____

What activities take place in this park?

_____

_____

What steps did the town follow when planning the park's construction?

_____

_____

_____

_____

What steps did the town follow to build the park?

_____

_____

_____

_____

Go on to the next page to begin Exercise 3A.

Exercise 3A: Newsletter Article

Directions: For Exercise 3A, you will write a newsletter article for your school's summer newsletter. In your article, you will imagine you live in the year 2100 A.D. Explain the dangers of spending the summer in the sun. Use the ideas you wrote in the first pre-writing activity. Describe the dangers of exposure to the sun's rays. Use specific details and descriptions. Use words that make your meaning clear. Your article should be well organized. Write your article in the space provided.

The writing you do for Exercise 3A will be scored. Look at the box below. Checklist 3A shows what your writing must include to receive your best score.

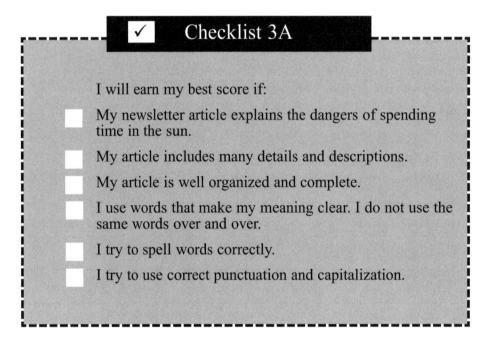

Checklist 3A

I will earn my best score if:

☐ My newsletter article explains the dangers of spending time in the sun.

☐ My article includes many details and descriptions.

☐ My article is well organized and complete.

☐ I use words that make my meaning clear. I do not use the same words over and over.

☐ I try to spell words correctly.

☐ I try to use correct punctuation and capitalization.

Use your pencil to write your article. You may erase, cross out, or make other editing changes to your work. You may not use a dictionary or thesaurus in your writing. Spell words to the best of your ability. Remember, writers often make changes as they work.

Exercise 3A: Newsletter Article

_____

_____

_____

_____

_____

_____

_____

_____

_____

_____

_____

_____

_____

_____

_____

_____

_____

_____

_____

_____

_____

_____

_____

_____

_____

_____

_____

_____

_____

_____

_____

_____

_____

_____

_____

_____

_____

_____

_____

_____

_____

When you finish writing your newsletter article, use the checklist to revise and edit your work. When you have finished checking your newsletter article, and you are satisfied with it, you may go ahead to the second activity, Exercise 3B.

Exercise 3B: Informational Essay

Directions: For Exercise 3B, you will write an informational essay. You will pretend you live in the year 2100 A.D. In your essay, you will offer many tips about how to protect yourself from the dangers of the sun's rays. Give ideas about how kids can have fun without being harmed by the sun's rays. Use the information you wrote in the second pre-writing activity. Your informational essay should be well organized and complete. Write your informational essay in the space provided.

The writing you do for Exercise 3B will be scored. Look at the box below. Checklist 3B shows what your writing must include to receive your best score.

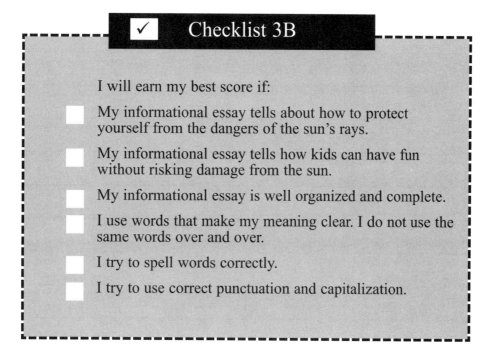

✓ **Checklist 3B**

I will earn my best score if:

☐ My informational essay tells about how to protect yourself from the dangers of the sun's rays.

☐ My informational essay tells how kids can have fun without risking damage from the sun.

☐ My informational essay is well organized and complete.

☐ I use words that make my meaning clear. I do not use the same words over and over.

☐ I try to spell words correctly.

☐ I try to use correct punctuation and capitalization.

Use your pencil to write your informational essay. You may erase, cross out, or make other editing changes in your work. You may not use a dictionary or thesaurus in your writing. Spell words to the best of your ability. Remember, writers often make changes as they work.

Exercise 3B: Informational Essay

_____

_____

_____

_____

_____

_____

_____

_____

_____

_____

_____

_____

_____

_____

_____

_____

_____

_____

_____

_____

When you finish writing your informational essay, use the checklist to revise and edit your work. When you have finished checking your informational essay, and you are satisfied with it, you may go ahead to the third activity, Exercise 3C.

Exercise 3C: A Set of Directions

Directions: For Exercise 3C, you will write a set of directions. Imagine you live in the year 2100 A.D. Your town built a park that is safe from the sun. Write a set of directions describing the building of this park. In your directions, explain how to build a park that is safe from the sun's rays. Use the ideas you wrote in the third pre-writing activity. Explain the steps needed in planning and building the town park. Use words that make your meaning clear. Your directions should be well organized and complete. Write your directions in the space provided.

The writing you do for Exercise 3C will be scored. Look at the box below. Checklist 3C shows what your writing must include to receive your best score.

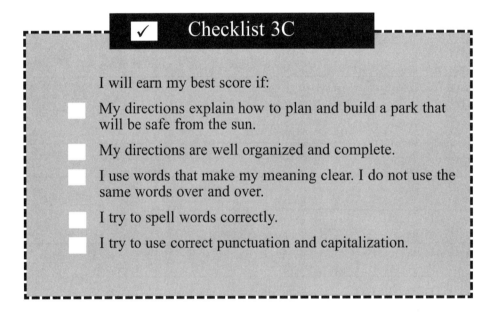

✓ Checklist 3C

I will earn my best score if:

- [ ] My directions explain how to plan and build a park that will be safe from the sun.
- [ ] My directions are well organized and complete.
- [ ] I use words that make my meaning clear. I do not use the same words over and over.
- [ ] I try to spell words correctly.
- [ ] I try to use correct punctuation and capitalization.

Use your pencil to write your directions. You may erase, cross out, or make other editing changes to your work. You may not use a dictionary or thesaurus in your writing. Spell words to the best of your ability. Remember, writers often make changes as they work.

Exercise 3C: A Set of Directions

_____

_____

_____

_____

_____

_____

_____

_____

_____

_____

_____

_____

_____

_____

_____

_____

_____

_____

_____

_____

_____

_____

_____

_____

_____

_____

_____

_____

_____

_____

_____

_____

_____

_____

_____

_____

_____

_____

_____

_____

_____

When you finish writing your directions, use the checklist to revise and edit your work.

Reading

Test 1

Before you begin Test 1, read
through the test-taking strategies
for Reading on the next page.
These strategies give you a chance
to practice answering short-answer
and extended-reponse items.

Test 1 questions begins on page 91.

Test-Taking Strategies for Reading
by Jolie Brams, Ph.D.

Read through the passage and the short-answer and extended-response items below.

One of the most exciting activities in sixth grade at Claypool School is the "Imaginative Invention Project." All sixth graders design, invent, and demonstrate creative inventions. Toward the end of the school year, there is an "Invention Day" filled with fun and activities. Tables are set up all around the auditorium and cafeteria, and each student demonstrates his or her invention. Parents help make this an exciting day by making and selling pizzas for all to enjoy. Fifth graders show off their cooking skills by making free ice cream for everyone. Mrs. Freshner, one of the sixth grade teachers, invites her husband to do magic tricks, and Mr. Silman, the principal, plays the guitar!

Everyone in the sixth grade wants to invent something that is "super special." Mrs. Freshner and the other teachers remind students this project is fun, but it could also make a student rich and famous. She reminds Claypool sixth graders that five years ago, a Claypool sixth grader invented a school supplies holder that hooks onto the end of someone's bed. The invention allows students to do homework and other projects while they are lying down and relaxing. A woodworking company in the town of Claypool thought this was a very good idea and made several hundred supply holders in their factory. This invention is now being sold in hardware stores and department stores in Claypool.

Almost every sixth grader wants to invent the best project, and many others hope to win the "most creative" or "most useful" award on Invention Day. Nearly everybody works together to help each other, and everyone has a lot of fun. That is, of course, except for the two nastiest bullies in the entire sixth grade: Robbie and Kim. They think they are popular and cool, although they are actually rude and unfriendly. They think they are the only kids in the sixth grade who know anything at all, and they spend most of their time putting other people down. The person they put down the most is Jacqueline. Ever since first grade, Robbie and Kim have rarely left Jacqueline alone for a minute. They tease her about her shyness, her thick glasses, and they make fun of her clothes. When Jacqueline was younger, she cried all the time because Robbie and Kim were mean to her, but now, as a more mature sixth grader, she just keeps to herself. Jacqueline has a few friends, but they are quiet too. All of them stay away from Robbie and Kim. Jacqueline often thinks to herself, "There is no way I could ever gain Robbie's and Kim's respect." After awhile, Jacqueline wonders why she even wants their respect or friendship at all.

Finally, Invention Day arrives. All the students are excited about showing off their inventions, but no one boasts more than Robbie and Kim. Robbie has created a new kind of "slime." Some of the slime is pink, some is green, and it looks terribly disgusting. You can pick up the slime in your hands and let it ooze through your fingers. Robbie has made the slime with soap, food coloring, and all sorts of other ingredients. Kim has created a project much like Robbie's. She mixed paint and glitter together in a squirt bottle. You can squirt the glitter paint right on paper and make beautiful designs. After setting up their displays, Robbie and Kim walk over to Jacqueline's table. In loud voices, they start making fun of Jacqueline. They criticize her "boring" invention. Jacqueline's table is covered with towels of different sizes, lined up neatly in boxes. Robbie and Kim notice the towels smell good. Kim says, "Who cares about a bunch of stupid towels anyway?"

Then, an interesting thing happens. Robbie and Kim are standing next to their table that holds the slime and the glitter paint. Suddenly, Mrs. Freshner's dog, Luther, escapes from the leash and comes barreling across the auditorium. The first table Luther hits is the one holding the slime and the paint. Before Mrs. Freshner can say, "Stop that dog!" slime and paint completely cover Kim's dress and Robbie's pants. Both of them complain loudly that their clothes are ruined, and they look like fools for Invention Day.

Suddenly, Jacqueline walks quietly out of a corner. In her hands are several of the towels Robbie and Kim made fun of just minutes earlier. Jacqueline quietly tells Robbie and Kim to use the towels to clean off their clothes. Almost immediately, a special cleaner on the towels begins to remove the slime and paint. Everyone's eyes are on Robbie, Kim, and Jacqueline. While the two nasty inventors are cleaning off their clothes, Jacqueline walks across the auditorium and back to her table. Applause breaks out. Invention Day changes Jacqueline's life.

Short-Answer Items

Describe two activities that take place on Invention Day to make the day enjoyable for everyone who participates.

1. _____
_____
_____

2. _____
_____
_____

The following is an example of a 2-point response:

Many things happen on Invention Day to make the day special for everyone. Mr. Silman plays the guitar and parents cook pizzas. Everybody can enjoy the sound of the guitar as they look at the students' inventions. Everyone can also enjoy eating the pizzas for lunch or even a snack. The aroma of the pizzas will probably make the auditorium and the cafeteria smell really good. Who wouldn't enjoy that?

Extended-Response Items

At the end of the story, Jacqueline walks across the auditorium while everyone is applauding. Describe how Robbie and Kim may be feeling at that moment. Then describe how you imagine Jacqueline could be feeling.

_____
_____
_____
_____
_____
_____
_____
_____

The following is a 4-point response:

When Jacqueline is applauded at the end of the story, Robbie and Kim probably feel embarrassed because they were so mean to Jacqueline. They also probably figure everyone in the auditorium saw the paint spill all over them. This will make them even more embarrassed. They also might feel ashamed they treated Jacqueline so badly, because the applause tells them the people are proud of Jacqueline for being nice to Robbie and Kim even though they didn't deserve it. Maybe Robbie and Kim will understand that being a bully isn't worth it, and people will not applaud you for it.

Jacqueline is probably proud of herself for helping Robbie and Kim because she was nice to them even though they were always mean to her. She might also think that maybe Robbie and Kim won't pick on her anymore because she helped them clean up the paint on their clothes. Also, Jacqueline is probably excited that her invention works really well and that all the people in the auditorium saw it work. Her invention will probably be the best invention at Invention Day.

Directions: Read the selection and answer the questions.

The Crystal Llama
by T. J. Perkins

Monica stared at the tiny figure her grandfather held in the palm of his hand. As the light touched it, it sparkled magically.

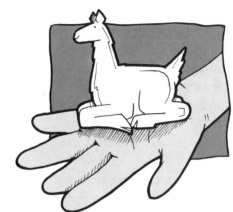

"This llama," her grandfather told her, "is carved out of crystal. When a crystal is given to someone dear, it gives the keeper good luck. A llama is a symbol of wealth and prosperity. So, you put the two together and you have yourself a fine good luck piece. Well, at least that's what the local people say, but that's only superstition." He paused and smiled at Monica.

"Is it for me?" Monica asked, astonished.

"Of course. Take it. Take good care of it. It came all the way from Peru."

Monica gingerly took the llama. It was beautiful. She kissed her grandfather on the cheek and ran excitedly to her room. She set the llama on her windowsill to watch it sparkle in the sunlight. "Hmm," she thought, "I wonder if my llama will bring me luck." Sixth grade had been kind of rough. It was hard making friends, keeping up with all the new challenges, plus, there was that part in the school play she had her heart set on. She felt she needed some luck.

The next morning she went to school carrying the crystal llama in her pocket. Everyone was extra nice to her. She made more friends, aced her test, and even found her calculator. Monica beamed as she patted her pocket. She decided to try out for the play.

The next day Monica tried out for the leading role in the play and got the part. Weeks went by, and every day, Monica felt more confident. Once, she accidentally left the llama at home, and nothing seemed to go right. When she kept the llama with her, everything was perfect.

The evening of the play arrived. Monica was very nervous, but with her crystal llama everything would be fine. Monica scrambled to get dressed. Her mother helped with her costume and makeup and cleaned up after the frenzied rush.

The nervous and excited bustle backstage gave Monica a stomachache.

"Hi, Monica," said her friend Crystal.

"Hi. I'm really scared," Monica revealed. "Hope I do okay."

"If you do as well tonight as you've done at rehearsal, I think everyone will love you," Crystal answered, with a big smile.

"Good old Crystal," Monica murmured to herself. "Crystal! Oh my! I forgot my llama!" She fumbled around in her costume pockets and finally felt a tiny lump. The lights dimmed, the announcer was speaking, the curtain went up, and the show began.

Monica spoke every line perfectly. She felt so confident, she forgot about being nervous and let herself become her character. The curtain fell as applause filled the auditorium.

Monica's proud parents greeted her after the performance. Monica said she couldn't have done it without the help of her lucky llama. She reached into her pocket and pulled out . . . her earrings! She felt a wave of panic. What happened to her llama?

At home, Monica raced to her room. She saw the crystal llama sitting on her dresser. She held it gently in her hand and sat on her bed. Just then her mother walked into her room.

"You found it," her mother said.

"I thought I had it the whole time. I thought this was the reason I did so well tonight," she said, looking up, with helpless eyes, at her mother.

"You did well tonight because it was in you all the time. Your confidence peaked, and you performed beautifully," she said.

"But, ever since Grandpa gave this to me, things have been so different, so right," Monica mumbled.

"I know it seems like that, but never put your trust in an object to bring you luck. Have trust and confidence in yourself, and a layer of 'luck' will shine around you all the time." With that, her mother kissed her on the forehead and left the room.

Monica smiled to herself, placed the crystal llama on her dresser, and got ready for bed.

The next morning, when she left for school, Monica left the crystal llama on her dresser. To her delight, her day went perfectly.

1. Why does Monica believe the llama brings her good luck?

   ○ A. Because her grandfather gave it to her.
   ○ B. Because it was made in Peru.
   ○ C. Because she had a great day when she first took the llama to school.
   ○ D. Because, with the llama in her pocket, she performed well in the school play.

2. How did owning the llama affect Monica's behavior?

   ○ A. She became quieter and more shy.
   ○ B. She was more confident of her abilities.
   ○ C. Monica was nicer to her parents.
   ○ D. Monica began to participate more in her classes.

3. What clues tell us Monica might not have her crystal llama with her on the night of the play?

    Support your answer with references to the story.

    _____

    _____

    _____

    _____

    _____

4. If you wanted to learn more about good luck charms, where might you look?

    ○ A. a book called *Witchcraft in the Middle Ages*
    ○ B. a video about magic
    ○ C. the magazine article, "Lucky Potions, Charms, and Talismans"
    ○ D. the owner of a magic store

5. The best type of person to recommend this story to would be whom?

    Support your answer with details from the story.

    _____

    _____

    _____

    _____

    _____

6. If one of your friends felt he or she could never succeed at anything, how would you respond?

   Give specific examples of how you would boost your friend's confidence.

   _____

   _____

   _____

   _____

   _____

   _____

Directions: Read the selection and answer the questions.

"Cheer, Cheer, Cheerful, Cheer"
by Deborah Tong

"Cheer, cheer, cheerful, cheer" is the sound of the Eastern Bluebird's song. The bluebird has much to be cheerful about lately. Thanks to a devoted group of volunteers, bluebird houses are being put up all over the United States. These houses offer bluebirds a safe place to nest and raise their young. Bluebird houses are often part of a bluebird trail. A bluebird trail is an area with at least five nesting boxes placed at least 100 yards apart. Through a nationwide system of bluebird trails, the North American Bluebird Society is working to increase the population of bluebirds.

Why worry about bluebirds? Bird lovers worry because of the rapid decline in bluebirds between 1900 and 1970. Since 1900, bluebirds have lost much of their natural habitat. This loss of habitat and nesting areas has made bluebirds more vulnerable to extreme weather, as well as to various pesticides used in agricultural areas. Environmentalists worried the cheerful bird might become extinct. Beginning in the 1970s, bird lovers began organizing bluebird trails. These trails have helped to dramatically increase the population of bluebirds, but bluebirds are still in danger. Nonnative birds, such as house sparrows and European starlings, will often invade and ruin a bluebird nest. Urban sprawl is also decreasing the amount of habitat area available for the bluebird.

The bluebird still needs help. Bird lovers across the country are putting up nesting boxes in their backyards and at their schools, churches, farms, and golf courses. For an ideal bluebird trail, volunteers need to be aware of the following points:

- Bluebird houses should be made according to specific patterns. The entry hole should be one and one-half inches in diameter, to keep out most predators.
- Bluebird houses should be made of cedar or redwood, so they will weather well. Houses should not be painted.
- Boxes should be located in an open area, but near woods.
- Boxes should be up year-round and should be kept clean between nestings. Bluebirds will often make four nests in one year.
- Monitor nest boxes until the birds are two weeks old. Check for parasites and signs of predators.

With the help of thousands of bluebird lovers, the bluebird is making a comeback in America.

7. Which statement best summarizes this article?

   ○ A. Volunteers are helping to increase the bluebird population.
   ○ B. Since 1900, bluebirds have lost much of their natural habitat.
   ○ C. Bluebirds like to nest in boxes.
   ○ D. House sparrows are one of the bluebird's predators.

8. Imagine your class wants to build a bluebird trail near your school.

Where would you build the trail? How would you get permission and money for your trail?

_____

_____

_____

_____

9. Why are bluebirds unable to succeed without help from people?

    Use information from the article to support your answer.

    _____

    _____

    _____

    _____

    _____

    _____

10. For which person would this article be most useful and informative?

    ○ A. the director of the city's bluebird trails
    ○ B. a chemical company that makes pesticides
    ○ C. the science and nature instructor at a summer camp
    ○ D. the president of the local lumber company

11. Which of the following statements from the reading passage is an opinion, not a fact?

    ○ A. A bluebird trail is an area with at least five nesting boxes placed at least 100 yards apart.
    ○ B. Since 1900, bluebirds have lost much of their natural habitat.
    ○ C. The bluebird has much to be cheerful about lately.
    ○ D. Boxes should be up year-round and kept clean between nestings.

Directions: Read the selection and answer the questions.

Toast
by Kay Day

Simple construction of bread and jelly
loses balance on a harried morning
to tumble into the lap
of a nine year old

who dabs with a napkin,
smears his sleeve, then studies it
all day long at school.

His mother sweeps crumbs,
clears nooks and crannies of dust,
every so often pausing

to study the paper heart
stuck to the refrigerator door
with a piece of tape.

12. What is the main emotion expressed in this poem?

  ○ A. frustration
  ○ B. love
  ○ C. anger
  ○ D. excitement

13. What is the mood inspired by this poem?

_____

_____

_____

_____

14. The poem begins with a description of toast and ends with a description of a paper heart.

In the poet's view, how are these two items related?

_____

_____

_____

_____

Directions: Read the selection and answer the questions.

Poetry Assignment
by Jennifer King

I'm not good at poems because every time
I always get stuck when I try to write rhymes.
When I begin writing I have lots to say,
But the right words come out in the wrong way... on paper.
And then there's this other thing too,
Meter comes in and it throws me off too.
Whoops, there I go! I used "too" in there twice,
But the meter is better; this is sounding quite nice.
Hey! I just managed a couple of lines.
This poetry thing is working out fin...ally.
Well, that sort of worked, kinda.
If this keeps getting harder I might have a mind to
Stop trying to write this poem at all.
Maybe instead I can go to the mall.
All and mall. Those two words rhyme well!
Now things in this poem are starting to gel.
A couple more lines and my poem is done.
Poetry writing could almost be fun
If it wasn't for all of this rhyming and stuff.
There, I fought my way through it, but it was rough.
Not a bad piece of work, as far as poetry goes,
But I think the next time I'll be writing in prose.

15. Describe the difficulties faced by the poet as she tries to complete the poetry assignment.

   Give specific examples from the poem that communicate the challenges faced by the poet.

   _____

   _____

   _____

   _____

   _____

16. The eleventh line of the poem reads: "Well, that sort of worked, kinda."

   What does this sentence mean?

   ○   A. The poet has decided to find a new job.
   ○   B. The poet is happy to be finished writing the poem.
   ○   C. The poet has written a piece in which all the lines rhyme.
   ○   D. The poet is trying to write a poem with lines that rhyme, but she has not been
            completely successful.

17. The best type of person to recommend this poem to would be whom?

   Support your answer with details from the poem.

   _____

   _____

   _____

   _____

18. Which of the following conclusions is not supported by the information in the poem?

    ○ A. The poet tries to incorporate meter in her poem.
    ○ B. The poet has a hard time putting her many thoughts down on paper.
    ○ C. The poet considers not completing the poem.
    ○ D. The poet will never write again.

Directions: Read the selection and answer the questions.

A Bowl of Cherries
by Devorah Stone

"These cherry pits are like boulders," Richard announced. "How many more bowls do I have to eat to break the record?"

Sally looked up from her art book, "Two."

Sally and Richard lounged in the basement recreation room. Richard looked at the two bowls of cherries on the table. He counted all the stems.

"Remember the time limit," Sally said, "twenty bowls of forty cherries each in thirty-five minutes."

"I know!"

Two more bowls. He took the next bowl and picked up the reddest cherry. People all over the world would read about Richard Algeron breaking the cherry-eating record. Richard sighed.

Sally snapped her book shut, "Are you going to eat those cherries, or what?"

"I think I'll do the 'or what.' "

"All those wasted cherries," she said looking at the bowl. "What are you going to do now?"

Richard stood up. "Well I can sleep in a graveyard for ten nights in a row."

"Creepy."

Richard did not know what to do. He just knew he had to break a record. He had to get into the book. Ever since he could read, he loved records. How tall? How fast? How much?

Once, he convinced his father to let him sleep on the roof for forty nights. If it hadn't hailed on the twentieth night, he would be in that book.

Richard felt he had a chance to break an eating record. He ate bathtubs of ice cream, chocolate bars, lobsters, and cherries. He went to pie and shellfish eating contests. Once he won a pancake-eating contest. Still, the Guinness people told him he was two pancakes short of the record.

Richard's mother collected buttons. She was on the television show, "People Do the Darnedest Things." His father owned a collection of staplers, including a gold-plated one and the only stapler handcrafted in Outer Mongolia. Sally created art — collections of everyday objects in large sculptures.

"OK," Sally said, "We shouldn't let the cherries go to waste. I can transform them into art."

Richard watched Sally. She inspected each cherry and removed the pits from the plumpest. She pureed the cherries and mixed the puree with clear acrylic latex. Pressing a large brush on a massive canvas, she spread the red paint.

She stepped back and looked at it. She shook her head. "It needs something."

Sally was having an artistic crisis. Richard looked at the canvas.

"Buttons!" he said.

"Buttons?"

"And staples," he added.

"Where?" she asked.

"Everywhere. Thread rows of buttons and hang them with a stapler gun."

Sally shook her head. "Mother will never let me use her buttons."

"Just tell her you want to create a shrine to her buttons."

To Sally's surprise, Mrs. Algeron helped her daughter choose the finest buttons. Mr. Algeron offered various kinds of staples. Sally and Richard plotted the best design. Together the family worked on their masterpiece.

They strung all the two-holed buttons and four-holed buttons. Heavy coat buttons accented the work. Sally alternated bright and neutral buttons for "rhythmic harmony."

When the creation was finished, the Algerons threw a party. Their friends said the assemblage was interesting. A few called it fascinating. Sally's art teacher suggested they contact "People Do the Darnedest Things."

The television people showed old clips of Mrs. Algeron's button collection. Mr. Algeron talked about the importance of staplers in the development of Western Civilization. Sally demonstrated how to make "cherry paint."

"The cherries symbolize flavor, while the buttons and staples bind the canvas together." She told them, "Actually, the buttons and staples were my brother's idea."

"A family effort," the host beamed. He asked Richard, "What is your goal in life?"

"To eat my way into the *Book of Records*."

The television host laughed, "What Richard means is he wants to get into this book." He held up the record book. "Now tell me, how many times have you tried to get into the *Book of Records*?"

"Lots and lots of times. I've called them up at least every two weeks for the last five years."

"Well those folks who publish the *Book of Records* keep a record of everything, including how many times people try to get into their book. And Richard Algeron you have tried 135 times! You have tried more times than anyone else! Because of your persistence, you will be in their next book!"

Richard turned cherry red. He couldn't believe it!

19. The members of the Algeron family all have different interests.

   Why were they all willing to work together on the cherry masterpiece?

   ○ A. They wanted to help Richard get into the *Book of Records*.
   ○ B. They wanted to be on television.
   ○ C. Sally was hoping to win a prize for the artwork.
   ○ D. Different parts of the masterpiece interested different members of the family.

20. Richard always wanted to be in the *Book of Records*.

   Why was he so surprised when he finally beat a record?

   _____

   _____

   _____

21. Goals are very important to people.

   What is one of your goals? What have you done to try to achieve your goal?

   _____

   _____

   _____

   _____

   _____

22. What was the author's purpose for writing this story?

    ○ A. to prove it is impossible to get in the *Book of Records*
    ○ B. to show people will always be successful
    ○ C. to encourage people to work hard for their dreams
    ○ D. to demonstrate the useful qualities of cherries

23. Which statement best summarizes this story?

    ○ A. Richard Algeron works hard to set a new record in something, anything!
    ○ B. The Algeron family becomes famous for their work on the cherry masterpiece.
    ○ C. Sally Algeron works to become a famous artist.
    ○ D. Mr. and Mrs. Algeron are proud of the children and their efforts to set a new record.

Directions: Read the selection and answer the questions.

Tug Of War
by Beth Adams

"What have you got there?" Sarah Carpenter asked.

"A rock," Philip Graham answered.

She laughed. "I guess that's why you're the lead geologist on this mission."

He turned to face her. "When did you get here?"

"Last shuttle up. How have you been?"

"Not bad — busy. Are you my assistant for this mission?" he asked.

"Well, I wasn't sent to wash dishes," she laughed. "I did want the Venus mission, but I needed more training missions, so I was sent to Mars instead."

"You wanted the Venus mission?" he asked, as he gathered his equipment.

"Yeah. If all goes well on this mission, I'm headed for Venus in six months."

"Let's get back. We need to analyze these samples, and I need your help finishing some reports."

Philip and Sarah sat hunched over microscopes in their Martian station lab. The researchers and astronauts had begun calling it 'the Redrock Lounge.'

"See anything interesting?" he asked her.

"Nope." She sat back and stretched.

"Well, we have plenty of others to examine. We also have those soil samples and excavated rocks to check."

"Then I'll look at some of those," she told him as she placed a petri dish of Martian soil on the microscope platform. She gasped, "Philip, come here!"

"What have you found?"

"Look. What does that look like to you?"

He studied the sample. "Sarah, where was this found?"

She checked the roster. "North quadrant. Area 36."

Philip looked at the sample again. "I've never seen anything like this."

"Well, I have," she said, "but I saw it on Earth. I know exactly what this is and so do you."

"Yes," he said as he sat back in the chair and rubbed his face. "Let's check the other samples before we jump to any conclusions. This may be a fluke."

After checking the samples, Philip turned to her and said, "Found it in every soil and excavated sample I checked. You?"

"The same. Every soil and excavated sample was full of them, but no surface rocks contained these crystals." She looked at him. "What are we going to do?"

"Put it in our report," he replied.

"No. If we do that, who knows what will happen."

"What we've found is too important not to be included."

"Philip, if we put this in an official report, there will be chaos on Earth. We know why we're here and why we're being sent to Venus. We're supposed to see if precious metals exist on the planets. We have found the most precious metal known. I'm not putting this in my report. Our solar system won't be able to handle it."

"We've got our job to do. Any consequences are not our concern."

She grabbed his arm. "Yes they are! The planets in our solar system are set out in a specific order. If the mass of any planet is disturbed significantly, the whole solar system could be thrown out of whack. Each planet relies on the gravitational pull of the others to stay in balance. If Venus and Mars are mined for metals, their masses will be greatly upset. Earth could be pulled from its orbit by the disruption of gravitational pulls. We found these platinum crystals here on Mars, and it is likely that there are even greater deposits on Venus. Industries will be racing to space to mine the platinum."

"What do you think we should do?" he asked.

"Lie." She removed the last sample from the microscope.

"This will cost the space agency billions."

"Who cares? There's more than money at stake here. I happen to have a family on Earth that I love more than anyone or anything. I'm not going to risk Earth being pulled apart during a tug of war between the sun and Jupiter just so some company on Earth can strip mine Venus and Mars to get rich off these crystals."

"OK," he said. "We'll falsify our reports. We'll have to counterfeit some samples."

"Ladies and gentlemen," the space agency representative began, "we sent two of our country's most brilliant geologists to Mars to look for precious minerals. Traces of platinum do exist on Mars. However, the planet lacks sufficient platinum crystals to consider establishing any mining operations on Mars. Now, if you have any questions, I'm sure Dr. Carpenter or Dr. Graham will be able to answer them for you."

One woman raised her hand. "If you didn't find sufficient platinum crystals on Mars, what did you find?"

Philip smiled at the woman and answered, "Rocks. Lots of rocks."

24. One of the themes of this story concerns the delicate balance of nature.

Why do you think the author set this story on Mars rather than on Earth?

_____

_____

_____

_____

25. We have all been taught not to tell lies.

Why did the author decide to have her characters lie to the public at the end of the story?

○ A. She wants readers to know that lying is acceptable.
○ B. Philip and Sarah decide that a lie would be acceptable if it meant saving the Earth.
○ C. Philip and Sarah decide not to lie, since a lie would be dishonest.
○ D. Philip and Sarah want to make money by selling the results of their research to a company.

26. Which statement best summarizes this story?

○ A. Two scientists discover platinum crystals on Mars and must decide whether to share their discovery with the public.
○ B. Two scientists disagree on how to conduct their research on Mars.
○ C. Two scientists go to Mars to find precious minerals.
○ D. Two scientists use their Martian research to become rich and famous.

27. If you wanted to learn more about the planets in our solar system, which of the following resources would not be helpful?

   ○ A. *The Milky Way and Beyond: Exploring the Galaxies of the Universe*
   ○ B. *An Introductory Guide to the Solar System*
   ○ C. "Could There Be Life on Other Planets?"
   ○ D. "Could Humans Survive on Another Planet?"

Note: Questions 28 through 31 do not refer to a passage.

28. Which of the following magazine articles would be most likely to include information about the childhood of golfer Tiger Woods?

   ○ A. "Tiger Woods: Breaking the Record at the U.S. Open 2000"
   ○ B. "The Top Five Golfers Today"
   ○ C. "The Life and Times of Tiger"
   ○ D. "Lions, and Tigers, and Bears"

29. Your best friend recommended a book and you loved it. You would like to read another book similar to it.

   Which of the following is not a good way to select a similar book?

   ○ A. ask your friend for another recommendation
   ○ B. ask the librarian for another book by the same author
   ○ C. search the library computer for books on similar subjects
   ○ D. ask your father what his favorite book was when he was your age

30. You and your classmates have been asked to make a display about what your school was like thirty years ago. You need to find some 30-year-old photographs of the school, its students, and its teachers.

   Which of the following would not be a good source?

   ○ A. the parents and grandparents of your classmates
   ○ B. the school library
   ○ C. an encyclopedia
   ○ D. some of the older teachers at school

31. For a school project, you need to find information about women pirates.

Which of the following would be most helpful?

- ○ A. a book titled, *Pirates of the Seven Seas*
- ○ B. the magazine article, "Women of the Sea: History's Forgotten Pirates"
- ○ C. the Internet site, "Fun Facts about Pirates and their Loot"
- ○ D. the novel, *Treasure Island* by Robert Louis Stevenson

Directions: Read the selection and answer the questions.

Letterboxing
by Deborah Tong

From the hilltop you shall see
A beautiful, ancient, live oak tree.
The steps that you will due east pace
Equal the miles in a marathon race.
Now turn to face the northwest quarter
Ten paces back, not any shorter.
Beneath the spot to watch for whales,
You'll find my book to tell your tales.

Sounds like a clue to buried treasure, doesn't it? Well, it is! It is a letterboxing clue. Letterboxing is an activity that is becoming popular in the United States. Popular in Britain since 1854, the first letterboxes were not planted in the United States until the 1980s. Letterboxing is a special treasure hunt that is fun for kids and adults.

Letterbox hunters are good at reading maps, using a compass, and deciphering clues. They tend to enjoy hiking, beautiful scenery, and the challenge of hunting for "treasure."

So, how do you participate in letterboxing? First of all, you need to find a clue to a letterbox in your area. Most clues are posted on the Internet at the Letterboxing North America web site. Some clues are hidden with other letterboxes, and other clues are only available by word-of-mouth. For your hunt, you will need a pencil, a compass, a small unlined notebook, an ink pad, and your personal rubber stamp. Your rubber stamp is best if it is homemade, then it is truly your "signature." Next you need to get to the starting point for your hunt.

Once you are ready to begin, you need to decipher your clues. Some clues are very precise directions: walk 100 yards due south and you will see the old stone wall. Other clues might be in riddles, in the form of a puzzle, or perhaps a secret code. Once you have deciphered your clue, you will begin your hike to the "treasure."

Most letterboxes are hidden in scenic areas so hunters will enjoy a pleasant day. When you find your letterbox, it will be a small, waterproof container. Inside, you will find a small notebook, a rubber stamp, and perhaps a few "goodies" or momentos. From the supplies you brought with you, take out your personal rubber stamp and ink pad. Ink your stamp, and stamp it in the book found in the letterbox. You may also write about your adventure finding the box and tell where you are from. It's fun to read the stories of those who found the letterbox before you!

Next, ink the stamp you found in the letterbox and stamp your own notebook. Again, you might write about the adventure of finding the box, how you deciphered the clues, and so on. If your letterbox has "goodies" you may take one, as long as you put something back in its place. Return the letterbox materials just as you found them, so they will be ready for the next hunter!

Soon, your notebook will have a collection of stamps to show your letterboxing skills and adventures. What next? Try hiding a letterbox of your own. Choose a scenic area on public land. Hide your letterbox where no one will find it unless they have your clues. Create your clues, and post them on the Internet. It will be fun to visit your box and see who has been there!

32. The best person to recommend this article to would be someone

- A. who spends all day watching television.
- B. who enjoys puzzles and outdoor activities.
- C. who drives a car to visit the next door neighbor.
- D. who is skilled at carving rubber stamps.

33. In this article, the author's purpose is

- A. to entertain the reader with anecdotes about letterboxing.
- B. to encourage Americans to hide letterboxes in every town.
- C. to remind people to hide letterboxes only on public property.
- D. to provide an introduction to letterboxing.

34. Which of the following is an opinion of the author?

- A. "It's fun to read the stories of those who found the letterbox before you."
- B. "The first letterboxes were not planted in the United States until the 1980s."
- C. "Most letterboxes are hidden in scenic areas so hunters can enjoy a pleasant day."
- D. "Most clues are posted on the Internet at the Letterboxing North America web site."

35. Why does the author begin this article with a riddle?

    ○ A. to entertain the reader
    ○ B. to make the reader think the article is a poem
    ○ C. to introduce the subject of riddles
    ○ D. to introduce something fun about the hobby of letterboxing

36. Based on the article, does letterboxing sound like an activity you would enjoy?

    Why or why not?

    _____

    _____

    _____

    _____

Directions: Read the selection and answer the questions.

Truffles
by Deborah Tong

    If legend is true, truffles have been loved by the Ancient Greeks and Romans, kings, presidents, popes, and actors. They are also loved by pigs, dogs, and the people who live in the countries of the Mediterranean and sell truffles at great profit!

    Truffles are underground mushrooms, known as tubers. They grow only in certain climates, in certain soils, and near certain types of trees, especially oaks. Truffles look like a small, chocolate or white colored brain, since the outer skin of the truffle is well-sculpted.

The most common truffles in the gourmet world are the white, black, summer, and winter truffles. Truffles have a distinctive aroma and are best eaten raw with mild foods so you can fully enjoy their flavor. Each year in France and Italy, you can attend many festivals devoted to the truffle.

The tricky part about truffles? Finding them. Throughout the centuries, truffles have been hunted using sows (female pigs). The sows, however, were difficult to train and loved to eat the truffles. Truffle hunters quickly learned that a well-trained dog would find truffles easily and would not be as eager to eat them!

Truffle hunters and their dogs head for the woods during truffle hunting season. The season is designed so truffles are picked at their ripest. Hunters cannot sell truffles out of season. Truffle hunters look near oak or hazelnut trees for areas where the ground has little vegetation. When the truffle grows underground, it disturbs the soil so few other plants will grow near it. Next, the hunter allows the dog to sniff the area to determine if truffles are growing. When truffles are found, they are dug up, cleaned off, and wrapped in paper or cloth.

Truffle hunters sell their harvest to local markets and restaurants. Some truffles are exported to other countries. In the United States, you can buy four ounces of fresh summer truffles for $32; a one-ounce jar of whole winter truffle costs $35! Truly, truffles are the food of kings!

37. What is the author's purpose in writing this article?

  - ○ A. to explain the horticultural differences between the various types of truffles
  - ○ B. to discuss the various legends associated with truffles
  - ○ C. to encourage readers to try truffles
  - ○ D. to briefly explain growing, hunting, and eating truffles

38. Which statement best summarizes this article?

  - ○ A. Truffles are gourmet mushrooms found underground and are usually hunted by dogs.
  - ○ B. Truffles grow mostly in Italy and France and are very expensive in the United States.
  - ○ C. Sows love to hunt for truffles, but they also like to eat them!
  - ○ D. Most truffles are found near oak or hazelnut trees.

39. What is meant by the last sentence in the article: "Truly, truffles are the food of kings!"

  - ○ A. Throughout history, many kings have enjoyed eating truffles.
  - ○ B. Truffles are very expensive and not everyone can afford to buy them.
  - ○ C. In ancient times, only royalty was allowed to eat truffles.
  - ○ D. You should always serve truffles when you have royalty to dinner.

40. Based on the information in this article, do you think you would like to eat truffles?

    Why or why not?

    _____

    _____

    _____

    _____

41. Which of the following statements from the reading passage is an opinion, not a fact?

    ○ A. "The season is designed so truffles are picked at their ripest."
    ○ B. "Truly, truffles are the food of kings!"
    ○ C. "Each year in France and Italy, you can attend many festivals devoted to the truffle."
    ○ D. "They [truffles] grow only in certain climates, in certain soils, and near certain types of trees, especially oaks."

End of Reading Test 1

Reading

Test 2

Directions: Read the selection and answer the questions.

Janice Darlene
by Ella Arden

Daddy came home from the hospital, and Momma said he didn't remember some things. I didn't think those things included us, but they did. Daddy shuffled into the house, looking tired and unsure of himself. His shoes dragged over the floor in a way I knew would make Momma cringe. He was wrecking her mop job, but Momma didn't say a word. She just kept her hand on his arm, helping him up the stairs to their room.

I stayed in the kitchen, nibbling my thumbnail. Upstairs, I could hear Momma's muffled voice. Two solid thunks told me Daddy's shoes had been kicked off. At least he remembered how to do that.

I crept up the stairs. The door to my parents' room stood open a little, and I listened to Momma's chatter. I could see Daddy sitting on the edge of the bed. He stared into space, while Momma hurried around him, unpacking his bag. Daddy didn't watch her; he just stared straight ahead, worrying the white cotton bedspread between his fingers. It was the only movement he made until Momma dropped a shoe.

Daddy turned to look. He wasn't upset at the sound, just curious. It seemed like he'd never heard a shoe fall before. Momma looked back at him; I could see half of her face and half of his through the door. One was sad, the other was curious.

Momma tried to smile, but she started crying. Daddy let go of the bedspread and held his hand out to her. It looked the way it always had, Daddy hugging Momma, but it wasn't the same. Daddy didn't remember holding her like that when Ronald fell and broke his ankle. He didn't remember holding her tight when I rode Curly for the first time. Momma said all of that was gone and that Daddy would have to build new memories with us.

Daddy didn't look like he really wanted to do that, though. He looked like he wanted to run away and hide. Momma said the doctors weren't positive how it had happened; Daddy had been driving home one minute, and the next, the car was on its roof in the ravine near the Carver farm. Daddy wasn't given a choice in forgetting stuff.

The next day Daddy was more energetic. Momma taught him how to use the lawn mower again, and he spent the morning working in the back yard. I watched Daddy from my window. Daddy looked normal from this distance; he walked straight and proud, sweat shining on his face and arms. Once, the lawn mower stopped running, and he cursed a storm while he fixed it. That was the Daddy I knew.

Around lunchtime, Daddy told Momma he'd mow the front yard after he ate and napped. Daddy ate with me, then left, but not before putting his plate in the sink and throwing his napkin away. Momma watched him like she couldn't believe it. I couldn't believe it either. The back door clicked against the frame as he left; I stood there, watching him through the screen as he crossed the lawn and got into the hammock.

Later, the screen door opened, then slammed shut with a bang. I slid off my chair and went to him. His hand was as I remembered it, big and callused, but warm. He smelled of grass and sweat, and I thought his hand still tingled from the mower.

Daddy closed his hand around mine and smiled down at me. When I tugged on his hand, Daddy came with me. He sat at the table, and I got him a glass of cold water. I stood next to him, watching him drink the entire glass of water in one long gulp.

"Thank you, Janice," he said.

I frowned. He wasn't getting our names right, so maybe what he needed was for me to help him with things like that.

"I'm Janice Darlene," I said. "No one ever calls me Janice."

He nodded slowly, then said my name, carefully sounding it out. He looked at me when he finished, and I nodded that he'd gotten it right. If he didn't know our names, then maybe I should show him other stuff, like the house. Momma said that anything could trigger Daddy's memory, so it was important we surround him with familiar things. I tried to imagine what it would be like to be among people I didn't know, in a house I couldn't remember. It was probably like the way I felt the first day I went to school.

1. Why does Janice Darlene seem nervous about her father coming home from the hospital?

_____

_____

_____

_____

2. Which of the following best describes the father's attitude in this story?

    ○ A. excited to see his family
    ○ B. sarcastic
    ○ C. eager to please
    ○ D. stubborn and angry

3. Which of the following excerpts from the story indicates the point when Janice Darlene realizes she can help her father readjust to life at home?

    ○ A. "Two solid thunks told me Daddy's shoes had been kicked off. At least he remembered how to do that."
    ○ B. "Daddy turned to look. He wasn't upset at the sound, just curious."
    ○ C. "It looked the way it always had, Daddy hugging Momma."
    ○ D. "He nodded slowly, then said my name, carefully sounding it out. He looked at me when he finished, and I nodded that he'd gotten it right."

4. Imagine someone in your family has lost his or her memory.

    How would you help this person feel comfortable in your home? What would you do to help this person remember his or her old life?

    _____

    _____

    _____

    _____

    _____

    _____

5. Which of the following sentences best summarizes this story?

    ○ A. Janice Darlene realizes her father might not remember her, but they can create new memories together.
    ○ B. Momma is excited Daddy does his own dishes now.
    ○ C. Daddy is scared at home and wishes he were still in the hospital.
    ○ D. Daddy works around the house so everyone will like him.

6. Daddy is shown to be a kind, caring man because he hugs Momma when she is crying.

   Write two other ways the reader knows Daddy is kind and caring.

   _____

   _____.

7. If you wanted to find information about how to help someone with memory loss, which of the following would be the best resource?

   ○ A. "The Dog Ate My Homework, and Other Excuses for Forgetting Assignments"
   ○ B. *Do I Know You? Helping Loved Ones to Recover Memories*
   ○ C. "Forget It! Dealing With Rebellious Children"
   ○ D. *Memoirs of a Nation: Exploring the History of America*

Directions: Read the selection and answer the questions.

Flintknapping
by Deborah Tong

Have you ever found an arrowhead in a freshly plowed field? In Ohio, most of the Native Americans made their arrowheads from a rock called flint. The process of making stone tools and arrowheads is known as flintknapping. Today, many craftspeople practice the art of flintknapping. Some flintknappers use their skills to create reproductions of ancient arrowheads, knives, and tools. Many flintknappers create more modern "artifacts," such as jewelry, hunting knives, and decorative objects.

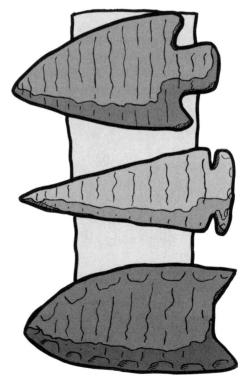

Flintknappers might be self-taught, or they may take classes in the craft. There are flintknapping classes and conferences throughout the country. A flintknapper begins with a piece of flint, other stones, or even coral. The stone is shaped using one of three methods: percussion flaking, pressure flaking, or indirect percussion. The flaking methods involve chopping or prying flakes of stone off by using hammerstones or deer antlers. With indirect percussion, the flintknapper hits a punch placed on the edge of the stone being worked.

By using hammerstones (rocks that fit well in the hand) and deer antlers, a flintknapper can shape a piece of stone very precisely. Modern flintknappers also use copper-tipped tools for shaping the stone. When a stone is near completion, a flintknapper will use sandstone to sharpen the edges of arrowheads and knives.

Modern flintknappers practice an ancient skill. Some craftspeople use only the ancient methods and create only accurate replicas of ancient tools. Other flintknappers have introduced modern tools into the craft and will produce modern jewelry, knives, and decorations in addition to replicas of ancient tools.

8. What purpose does the first sentence serve in terms of the whole article?

    ○ A. It describes the process of flintknapping.
    ○ B. It gets the reader personally involved in the article.
    ○ C. It requires that the reader has lived on a farm.
    ○ D. It indicates that the setting of the story is in Ohio.

9. How do the techniques of some modern flintknappers differ from those of the early Native Americans?

    ○ A. Modern flintknappers use electric machinery to produce their work.
    ○ B. Modern flintknappers might use rocks other than flint.
    ○ C. Modern flintknappers might use copper-tipped tools.
    ○ D. Modern flintknappers produce only accurate replicas of ancient tools.

10. Which of these sentences best summarizes this article?

    ○ A. Flintknapping is an ancient craft.
    ○ B. Flintknapping is a difficult, precise kind of work.
    ○ C. Flintknappers today use many of the ancient methods to create replicas and decorative objects.
    ○ D. Most modern flintknappers learn their skills from family members.

11. Which of the facts in the selection did you find most unusual or interesting?

    Explain why.

    _____

    _____

    _____

    _____

    _____

    _____

12. This article would be useful as

    ○ A. a brief introduction to flintknapping.
    ○ B. a set of directions for making a flint arrowhead.
    ○ C. a resource for someone seeking a class in flintknapping.
    ○ D. a comparison between ancient and modern jewelry making techniques.

13. Which book would most likely give more information about the ideas presented in
    this selection?

    ○ A. *The Encyclopedia of Ancient Crafts*
    ○ B. *Moundbuilders and Flintknappers: Everyday Life of Ohio's Early Native Americans*
    ○ C. *The Year 2000 Listing of Flintknapping Festivals*
    ○ D. *Tools of the Trade: Ancient and Modern Spears and Arrowheads*

Directions: Read the selection and answer the questions.

Beach Soup
by Kay B. Day

Only a child knows the true meaning of the ocean,
that shells wash up to be collected
and tossed into a hole in the sand
mixed with sea water, blended well
and served up to taste on a yellow plastic shovel
to a parent
who proclaims,
"Delicious!"

Only a child dashes into surf
to man an inflated raft
that sails a dangerous course
amid pirates and sea monsters
that nip at tender heels.

Only a child can follow the wind
blown across water from some faraway place
and, filled with the joy that innocence knows,
select the perfect shell to carry home to winter.
When the ground is cold and still and hard,
a tiny hand retrieves the shell,
cups it to the ear
as mystical waves lap from a distance
carrying the smell of beach soup delectable
and making the frost of winter melt
slowly and surely as we stir.

14. This poem takes place in two settings: the beach and the home in winter.

To the child, how are these settings similar? How are they different?

_____

_____

_____

_____

15. The best person to recommend this story to would be someone

   ○ A. who has young children.
   ○ B. who enjoys vacations in the mountains.
   ○ C. who likes to cook.
   ○ D. who is interested in marine animals.

16. This poem discusses the "true meaning" of the ocean but uses a lot of imaginative vocabulary: "faraway," "mystical," etc.

How does this imaginative vocabulary define the "true meaning" of the ocean?

_____

_____

_____

_____

17. Based on the poem, which of the following statements most likely is not true?

   ○ A. The child enjoys making up imaginary stories about the ocean.
   ○ B. The poet enjoys watching children play at the beach.
   ○ C. The child visits the beach in summer but forgets about it in winter.
   ○ D. The child carries memories of the beach with him all year long.

18. What is the main theme or message of this poem?

- ○ A. Adults do not enjoy spending time at the beach.
- ○ B. Children have wonderful imaginations.
- ○ C. Winter is a depressing time of year.
- ○ D. It is fun to listen to the sound of the surf in a shell.

19. The poet defines winter as a time "when the ground is cold and still and hard."

How does this line emphasize the importance of the beach in the child's life?

- ○ A. Winter and summer offer equal opportunities for the child to have fun.
- ○ B. Winter is the opposite of the warm, windy, wavy time of summer.
- ○ C. Summer is the only season during which the child can enjoy the beach.
- ○ D. The child is unable to use his imagination during the winter.

Directions: Read the selection and answer the questions.

East Meets West: A Quick Guide to Showing Your Best Table Manners in Japan
by Deborah Tong

Imagine this scene: You are visiting some new friends in Japan. They have asked you to join them for dinner at a fancy restaurant with several of their friends. You need to make a good impression, but you are not sure about proper Japanese table manners. The chart that follows will give you a quick guide to Japanese etiquette. Comparisons are made with proper table manners in the United States. Good luck!

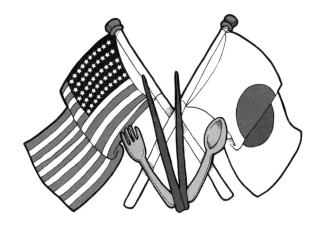

When in Japan...	When in the USA...
1. For a napkin, use a paper napkin or handkerchief you have brought with you.	1. Place your napkin in your lap before you begin eating or drinking.
2. Wait until all food is on the table and everyone is seated before beginning. Begin eating after someone says, "Itadakimasu" (I will receive).	2. Grace may or may not be said. Begin eating after the hostess takes her first bite.
3. Use chopsticks for all foods except: • use a knife and fork for Western food • use a spoon for eating curry rice • use a ceramic spoon to eat soup	3. Use appropriate silverware (spoon for soup, fork for salad). If you have multiple forks or spoons, work from the outside toward your plate.
4. Place the lid of your rice bowl upside down and to your left. The lid of your soup bowl is placed upside down and to your right.	4. Your glass is located to your right. Your bread plate is to your left.
5. Do not stick chopsticks vertically into rice. This is a sign of mourning for the dead and is considered bad luck for the living.	5. Meals may be served one course at a time.
6. Do not wave your chopsticks around while talking. Put them on the chop-stick rest when you are not eating.	6. Do not wave your silverware around while talking. Place your knife along the top of your plate and your fork in the four o'clock position.
7. For appropriately sized dishes, hold the dish in your hand while eating. Lift the dish to your chest if eating soup or rice to avoid spills.	7. When eating soup, you may tip your bowl away from you to get the last bits of soup.
8. When eating noodles or soup, it is okay to make slurping sounds.	8. It is impolite to make any eating noises.
9. When you finish eating, put your chop-sticks on the chopstick rest. The tips of the chopsticks should point to your left.	9. When finished eating, place your fork and knife together in the four o'clock position.
10. The meal ends with, "Gochiso sama deshita" (Thank you for the feast).	10. The meal ends when the host suggests everyone rise from the table.

20. What purpose does the chart serve?

  ○ A. The chart makes learning Japanese table manners quick and easy.
  ○ B. The chart allows the reader to compare the table manners of different countries.
  ○ C. The chart makes it more complicated to understand Japanese table manners.
  ○ D. The chart provides a step-by-step checklist for everything you need to know for eating in Japan.

21. Why does the author compare Japanese table manners with American table manners?

  ○ A. Because the Japanese are more polite than the Americans.
  ○ B. It is interesting to notice the differences in the two sets of table manners.
  ○ C. It is helpful to learn something new by comparing it with something you know.
  ○ D. It is useful to know you must take your own napkin to dinner in Japan.

22. Based on the information in the article, which of the following is most likely true?

  ○ A. It is very difficult to eat politely in a foreign country.
  ○ B. Although not polite in Japan or America, it is acceptable in some countries to wave your silverware around while talking.
  ○ C. Many cultures use specific utensils for specific courses or foods.
  ○ D. Meals in the United States and Japan both begin with a blessing.

23. The chart follows a logical order.

  Explain this order. Why is it used by the author?

  _____

  _____

  _____

  _____

24. Who would benefit most from this article?

    ○ A. someone with fairly good American table manners
    ○ B. someone with fairly good Japanese table manners
    ○ C. someone who never plans to leave the United States
    ○ D. someone who plans to travel to Japan

25. Imagine you are visiting Japan.

Would you want your hosts to correct your manners? Why or why not?

_____

_____

_____

_____

26. If you were to travel to Japan, which of the following books would not be helpful?

    ○ A. *Traveler's Guide to Tokyo, Japan*
    ○ B. *Everyday Chinese Cooking*
    ○ C. *Learn Japanese in 45 Minutes a Day*
    ○ D. *Japanese Customs, Holidays, and Celebrations*

Directions: Read the selection and answer the questions.

Mr. Davis Yells
by Barbara Mack

Juan dribbled the ball toward the hoop and went to take his shot. Marcus jumped to block him; the two collided in midair, and the ball went flying. It rolled off the driveway and out of Marcus' yard. It didn't come to a halt until it landed under Mr. Davis' peach tree. Juan and Marcus groaned. Neither of them wanted to go into Mr. Davis' yard and get the ball.

Mr. Davis moved in a month ago, and he yelled all the time. He yelled at his wife, and he yelled at his dog. He yelled at Marcus and Juan because they'd been inline skating on the sidewalk and had fallen into his flower bed and accidentally trampled his flowers. He'd scared them so badly, they'd skated away while he was still yelling.

Marcus walked over to Mr. Davis' yard and looked around. He didn't see Mr. Davis anywhere. He would just run into the yard, pick up the ball, and sneak back home as fast as he could. Who wanted to listen to all that screaming?

Just as Marcus leaned down to pick up the basketball, he heard a screen door creak as it opened. When he looked up, Mr. Davis was standing by the back door, drying his hands on a dish towel. "Don't eat those peaches!" Mr. Davis yelled. "Don't eat those peaches, Marcus!"

Marcus scooped up his basketball and ran away as Mr. Davis shouted for him to come back, but Marcus pretended he didn't hear him. When Marcus got back to his own yard, Juan told him he didn't want to play basketball anymore. He was going home.

"I wasn't going to eat his stupid old peaches anyway," Marcus thought resentfully as he sat alone on his back step and kicked at a clod of dirt. "It's not like Mr. Davis doesn't have enough peaches on that tree to feed the whole neighborhood, either. Why does he have to act that way?"

When Marcus heard his mother calling him, he went inside, letting the door slam behind him. His stomach cramped when he noticed Mr. Davis standing beside his mother, and his mouth twisted. This was so unfair. He was going to be in big trouble all because of a peach he wasn't going to eat.

Marcus' mouth fell open when his mother began explaining what Mr. Davis wanted. Mr. Davis didn't want him to eat the peaches because they weren't ripe yet, and unripe fruit can give you a stomachache. He also wanted to tell Juan and Marcus to be careful around his flowers because he'd found a snake hole. He was afraid the snake was still around somewhere, and he didn't want the boys to be bitten.

When Mr. Davis turned to smile at Marcus' mother, Marcus' smile grew even wider. As Mr. Davis turned his head, Marcus had spotted a hearing aid in Mr. Davis' ear.

27. Why does the author include the final paragraph in this story?

How does this paragraph relate to the rest of the story?

_____

_____

_____

_____

28. Which of the following sentences best summarizes this story?

○   A. Marcus and Juan are afraid of Mr. Davis.
○   B. Marcus' mother wants him to be kind to their new neighbor.
○   C. Mr. Davis is a mean, cranky neighbor who scares all the neighborhood children.
○   D. Marcus learns he has misunderstood his new neighbor.

29. If you wanted to recommend this story to someone, who, of the following, would be a good choice?

○   A. someone who likes to play basketball
○   B. someone who has kind neighbors
○   C. someone who needs to learn to be more understanding of others
○   D. someone who likes to inline skate

30. How do Marcus' feelings about Mr. Davis change during the story?

Discuss at least two instances where Marcus' opinions about Mr. Davis change.

_____

_____

_____

_____

31. Imagine that Marcus wants to apologize to Mr. Davis for misunderstanding his good intentions. He has decided to make him a cookbook of recipes for peaches.

    Which of the following articles would not be a good resource for peach recipes?

    ○ A. "Just Peachy: Recipes for Summertime"
    ○ B. "Best Recipes for Different Peach Varieties"
    ○ C. "The Care and Feeding of Peach Trees"
    ○ D. "Peaches in the Morning, Peaches in the Evening, Peaches at Supper Time"

32. Which of the following statements best represents the main theme of this story?

    ○ A. Sometimes, neighbors are mean and cranky.
    ○ B. Don't judge people until you know them well.
    ○ C. Children should stay out of their neighbor's yards and gardens.
    ○ D. Yelling is an effective way to communicate.

Directions: Read the selection and answer the questions.

Thar She Blows!
by Deborah Tong

July 19, 2000

"There's a blow at 11 o'clock!" exclaimed the naturalist aboard our whale watching ship. "Looks like a fin whale. Notice the tall, narrow column erupting from the blowhole? We'll hold here for a moment and see if it surfaces again."

The morning had dawned chilly and cloudy, but the sun peeked through as we drove to a harbor in New Hampshire. Ten of us clambered aboard the whale watching vessel, eager to spot our first whales. We began the ride toward Jeffrey's Ledge, where several different whale species tend to feed during the summer. It would take almost two hours to get to the feeding grounds. We enjoyed our picnic lunch and the beautiful views of the Isles of Shoals, the New Hampshire and Maine coasts, and, further out, the sea and seabirds: sea gulls, petrels, and shearwaters.

About an hour into our trip, the naturalist spotted the first whale. A fin whale was feeding well west of Jeffrey's Ledge. We watched the whale spout, surface, and dive for about fifteen minutes. Fin whales are the second largest creatures on Earth (second to blue whales). This fin whale was about 60 feet in length — almost as long as our boat! After the whale headed into a deep dive, we continued toward Jeffrey's Ledge.

Fifteen minutes later, our naturalist announced another fin whale at two o'clock. To help passengers spot the whales, the naturalist used directions related to the hours on a clock. Twelve o'clock was straight ahead, three o'clock was to the starboard side (the right side), six o'clock was to the stern (the back), and nine o'clock was to port (the left side). This fin whale was one of the biggest — about 70 feet in length. It was awe-inspiring to watch something so huge make its way so easily through the water. We enjoyed watching the fin whale for some time, and then continued on to Jeffrey's Ledge. On our way, we caught a quick sighting of a minke whale. The minke whale looks like a dolphin, but it is larger and it usually travels alone, rather than in a group.

We still had not arrived at our destination when our naturalist spotted another species: Atlantic white-sided dolphins. It was thrilling to watch these agile, beautiful mammals move through the water. Although not as playful as the familiar bottlenose dolphin, these white-sided dolphins swam in a group, fed on fish, and chased the wake of another boat nearby. The dolphins were traveling in a group of 30 – 40, and presented a rare sight for whale-watchers.

Finally, Jeffrey's Ledge was upon us. The water there, 20 miles from shore, was about 100 feet deep. The area was filled with plankton, small fish, and nutritious krill. Whales congregate in this area for feeding during the summer. Baleen whales, such as the fin whale and the humpback whale, filter thousands of gallons of sea water through their baleen (long strings in their mouths). The water is pushed from their mouths and the food remains behind.

"Another blow at 12 o'clock! Notice the column of mist is shorter and wider than that of the fin whale. This is a humpback whale." We watched the humpback for about twenty minutes. It seemed to have its own pattern of swimming: surface and blow three times, then blow and dive on the fourth surfacing. As the humpback dove, it would push its tail into the air, so we saw several good views of both the back and the tail of the whale.

Humpback whales migrate great distances during the course of a year. In the winter, they will travel as far south as Venezuela. In the warm southern waters, they will give birth to their young, and raise them until they are ready to travel. During these four to five months, the humpback whales will eat nothing. The clear, beautiful waters are warm but hold little food for baleen whales. During the summer months, the humpback whales live in northern waters, mostly off the coasts of New England and Canada. For the summer season, the whales will eat all the food they need for the year, often spending 18 hours a day just eating!

It was an amazing day, even for our experienced naturalist! We had great views of both fin and humpback whales, a quick view of a minke whale, and great fun with a large pod of Atlantic white-sided dolphins. We had climbed aboard the ship in hopes of spotting our first whale, and we came ashore as experienced whale-watchers.

33. According to the information in the article, which of the mammals sighted is the smallest?

    ○ A. the Atlantic white-sided dolphin
    ○ B. the minke whale
    ○ C. the humpback whale
    ○ D. the fin whale

34. Which of the following statements is not a fact, but is an opinion of the author?

    ○ A. "It seemed to have its own pattern of swimming: surface and blow three times, then blow and dive on the fourth surfacing."
    ○ B. "Humpback whales migrate great distances during the course of a year."
    ○ C. "The morning had dawned chilly and cloudy, but the sun peeked through as we drove to a harbor in New Hampshire."
    ○ D. "It is awe-inspiring to watch something so huge make its way so easily through the water."

35. Which statement best summarizes this article?

    ○ A. The author spent a great day whale watching and was fortunate to spot three kinds of whales and one type of dolphin.
    ○ B. The article explains many important details about all the different whale species found in the waters off the coast of Florida.
    ○ C. Whale watching is a fun activity for families, and if you go, you will see three kinds of whales and one type of dolphin.
    ○ D. Whale watching is best done in a good sized ship, on calm seas, and off the coast of New Hampshire.

36. The best person to recommend this article to would be someone

    ○ A. who is afraid of the ocean.
    ○ B. who is interested in learning about large mammals.
    ○ C. who likes to go fly-fishing in mountain streams.
    ○ D. who is a professional ocean sailor.

37. In the article, the author expresses her excitement about seeing whales for the first time.

   Tell about a time you were excited to see or do something new to you. Include details to explain why this event was exciting for you.

   _____

   _____

   _____

   _____

   _____

   _____

38. According to the information in the article, which of the following statements is most likely true?

   ○ A. Fin whales are the largest animals on Earth.
   ○ B. Atlantic white-sided dolphins often travel alone, rather than in groups.
   ○ C. Humpback whales lose a lot of weight during the winter months.
   ○ D. Minke whales are endangered and are rarely spotted.

39. This article is written as a personal travel journal.

   Why has the author chosen this style?

   ○ A. to remember her whale watching trip
   ○ B. to share information about a whale watching trip in an informal style
   ○ C. to provide formal, detailed information about whale watching
   ○ D. to give the reader a glimpse of the people on the whale watching trip

40. How does the author describe the various mammals without making the article confusing?

   ○ A. She puts information about each mammal under a separate sub-heading.
   ○ B. She begins each new paragraph with information about a new mammal.
   ○ C. She organizes the article in the order of the trip and tells about each mammal as she saw it on the trip.
   ○ D. She scatters information about the various mammals throughout the article so the reader is never bored.

41. If you wanted to learn more about sea mammals, which of the following would not be a good resource?

   ○ A. the Internet site for the Center for Oceanic Research and Education
   ○ B. an article titled "The Princes of Whales: Baleen and Toothed Whales Rule the Sea"
   ○ C. a book called *Easy Identification of Whales, Dolphins, and Porpoises*
   ○ D. a video titled *Treasure Island: The Search for Treasure in the Deep Sea*

End of Reading Test 2

Mathematics

Test 1

Before you begin Test 1, read through the test-taking strategies for Mathematics on the next page. These strategies give you a chance to practice answering short-answer and extended-reponse items.

Test 1 questions begins on page 136.

Short-Answer Items

Austin's uncle has a pond near his farmhouse. There are no fish in the pond, but Austin would like to stock it with fish so he and his cousins can go fishing in the summer. Austin bought a book about trout and found a trout needs 30 cubic feet of water to be happy and healthy. What steps would Austin take to find out how many fish his uncle should buy to stock the pond? In the space below, list the first two steps Austin should take to find out how many fish he should buy according to the book he read.

_____
_____
_____
_____
_____
_____

This short-answer response does not ask you to find an answer. Instead, you are asked to share how you would think through the problem. The item does not ask you to write long or fancy sentences, only to jot down your ideas. You have found out the book that Austin read states fish need 30 cubic feet of room to live healthy lives. Your first step is to measure the length and width of the pond. Next, you need to find some way to measure the depth of the pond to find out square footage. Your short-answer may be:

1. First, Austin should measure the length and width of the pond.

2. Second, Austin should measure the depth of the pond. By finding these measurements, Austin could determine the volume of the pond. Austin should divide the pond's volume by 30 cubic feet to determine the number of trout his uncle should buy.

Remember your test-taking strategies. Read the question carefully so you understand what is being asked. You know the question has to do with the size of the pond and how many fish could comfortably live in the water. You also know you are not being asked a specific number but only how you would figure out this problem. You could use your pencil to draw a picture of a pond, so you could look at what you are thinking about. You might decide to draw vertical and horizontal lines to think about the length and width of the pond. You may even draw a three-dimensional pond to understand you need to also measure depth.

Extended-Response Items

Let's take the same question about Austin, his uncle, and stocking the fish pond. Suppose the question were changed.

The pond is 100 feet long by 30 feet wide by 10 feet deep. Austin's uncle only has enough money to buy 100 fish. Given what you know about the pond and the number of fish Austin's uncle can buy, does the number of fish Austin's uncle can afford exceed the number of fish that can live in the pond? Remember, Austin's book said one trout needs 30 cubic feet of water. Please show your problem solving and give your answer.

_____
_____
_____
_____
_____
_____
_____
_____
_____
_____
_____
_____
_____

In this extended-response question, you are asked to show numbers on paper. You can still use your pencil and diagrams to think through the problem, but you are asked to use complete mathematical equations as well as words to describe how you decided if Austin's uncle can fit 100 fish into the pond. Your response would look something like this:

Begin by calculating the volume of the pond:
30 feet wide x 100 feet long x 10 feet deep = 30,000 cubic feet

If each fish needs 30 cubic feet to be healthy:
30,000 cubic feet ÷ 30 cubic feet = 1,000 fish could live in the pond

I have shown that Austin's uncle could have as many as 1,000 fish in the pond. If he bought 100 fish, they would have plenty of room. The number of fish Austin's uncle can afford does not exceed the number of fish that can live happily in the pond.

1. Kim's square flower garden measures 3 ft. by 3 ft., or 9 sq. ft. She wants to plant more flowers this year, so she made her garden 6 ft. by 6 ft.

   How many more square feet of space will Kim have in her flower garden?

   ○ A. 9 sq. ft.
   ○ B. 36 sq. ft.
   ○ C. 27 sq. ft.
   ○ D. 18 sq. ft.

2. Julie is knitting an afghan. The afghan is made of 3" x 3" squares. On Tuesday, Julie's afghan measures 6" x 6".

   How many squares does the afghan contain?

   ○ A. 2 squares
   ○ B. 9 squares
   ○ C. 3 squares
   ○ D. 4 squares

3. Students take a 20 point quiz. There are 5 points given for each correct answer (n).

   Which equation is the correct one to use to find the grade (e) for each student?

   ○ A. $n = 5e$
   ○ B. $5 = n \times e$
   ○ C. $e = 5 \times n$
   ○ D. $e = 5 - n$

4. Greg earns $6.00 a day in the summer doing odd jobs as a handyman's assistant.

   If Greg works five days a week, how much does he earn in a week? How much will he earn in eight weeks?

   ○ A. $30.00; $240.00
   ○ B. $30.00; $480.00
   ○ C. $30.00; $48.00
   ○ D. $11.00; $88.00

136

5. Gia needs to save $150.00 for a vacation. She plans to babysit after school for
    $3.00 an hour.

    Write an equation to find the number of hours (*n*) Gia will have to work to reach her goal.

    ○ A. $3.00 x *n* = $150.00
    ○ B. $3.00 x $150.00 = *n*
    ○ C. *n* = $150.00 - $3.00
    ○ D. $150.00 = $3.00 – *n*

6. Which equation represents the statement "five less than twice the number
    symbolized by (*m*)?"

    ○ A. $5 - 2m$
    ○ B. $5(m - 2)$
    ○ C. $5 - m + 2$
    ○ D. $2m - 5$

7. Kurt has a 4.0 Grade Point Average in math at the end of the third grading period. His math
    grades to date for the fourth grading period are 89, 95, 98, 100, 88, 100, and 93. He needs
    an average of 93 or better in math to maintain his 4.0 GPA for this grading period. He
    already has an "A" in science.

    If Kurt wants to figure out if he has an "A" average in math, does this problem have
    enough information?

    Explain your answer.

    _____

    _____

    _____

    _____

8. Sunday is the best day for snack sales at the food court in the mall. Monday is usually a slow day. Gina sold $847.25 in snacks last Sunday and $1,212.75 this Sunday. How does this compare with last month's sales?

   Are you given enough information to solve the problem? What information is still needed? What information is unnecessary? Explain your answer.

   _____

   _____

9. Tom is beginning physical therapy that involves swimming laps in a heated pool. On Monday, he swam two laps. On Tuesday, he swam two laps. By Wednesday, he could swim three laps. He could only swim three laps on Thursday. On Friday, Tom's trainer set up a schedule. On Friday, Tom would swim two laps, and every other day, Tom would add one lap.

   If Tom swims Monday through Friday, on what day of the week will he first swim 6 laps?

   ○ A. Monday
   ○ B. Tuesday
   ○ C. Wednesday
   ○ D. Thursday

10. The National Junior Honor Society at King School is inducting 23 sixth graders. There are 14 eighth graders and 21 seventh graders who are already members of the society.

    If there are 16 more girls than boys in the society, how many boys are in the society?

    ○ A. 58
    ○ B. 42
    ○ C. 37
    ○ D. 21

11. The Music Department at Knight School plans to use a $5,000.00 grant to fund a field trip.

    If the expenses for the field trip will be $32.00 for each of the 155 students attending, will they have enough money?

    ○ A. Yes, but they will not have any money left over.
    ○ B. Yes, and they will have money left over.
    ○ C. No, they will not have enough to cover the trip.
    ○ D. There is not enough information to solve this problem.

12. Tim is a computer technician. He earns $36,720.00 a year.

    How much money does Tim earn each month?

    ○ A. $1,224.00
    ○ B. $3,060.00
    ○ C. $3,672.00
    ○ D. $1,530.00

13. Janna makes $3,060.00 a month before deductions. She has a total of $983.78 in deductions each month for taxes, insurance, and retirement.

    About how much money does Janna have to spend each week? Round your answer to the nearest ten.

    ○ A. $419.05
    ○ B. $2,080.00
    ○ C. $2,076.22
    ○ D. $520.00

14. Which answer choice correctly completes this number sentence?

    63.051 _____ 630.51

    ○ A. is equal to
    ○ B. is greater than
    ○ C. is less than
    ○ D. is less than or equal to

15. Mike ordered a party pizza for himself and two friends to eat. The tray of pizza was cut into 24 slices.

   If each boy ate one-third of the pizza, how many slices did each boy eat?

   ○ A. 4 slices
   ○ B. 6 slices
   ○ C. 8 slices
   ○ D. 10 slices

16. On 'hat day' at school, only 10 people in Lori's homeroom of 24 students remembered to wear hats.

   What fractional part, reduced to lowest terms, remembered to wear hats?

   ○ A. $\dfrac{5}{6}$

   ○ B. $\dfrac{5}{8}$

   ○ C. $\dfrac{5}{12}$

   ○ D. $\dfrac{10}{24}$

17. Sam received $320.00 in graduation gifts. He spent one-fourth of the money on a jacket.

   How much did the jacket cost?

   ○ A. $\dfrac{1}{4}$ of $320.00 = $40.00

   ○ B. $\dfrac{1}{4}$ of $320.00 = $60.00

   ○ C. $\dfrac{1}{4}$ of $320.00 = $80.00

   ○ D. $\dfrac{1}{4}$ of $320.00 = $100.00

18. Janet got an 80% on a math quiz.

What fractional part of the quiz did she have correct?

- ○ A. $\dfrac{1}{5}$

- ○ B. $\dfrac{2}{5}$

- ○ C. $\dfrac{3}{5}$

- ○ D. $\dfrac{4}{5}$

19. Which decimal would be correctly rounded to 14.588 if rounded to the thousandths place?

- ○ A. 14.58726
- ○ B. 14.58756
- ○ C. 14.58856
- ○ D. 14.58876

20. Put these fractions in order from least to greatest value.

$$\dfrac{1}{3} \qquad \dfrac{5}{6} \qquad \dfrac{1}{12} \qquad \dfrac{2}{3}$$

- ○ A. $\dfrac{1}{3} \qquad \dfrac{2}{3} \qquad \dfrac{5}{6} \qquad \dfrac{1}{12}$

- ○ B. $\dfrac{1}{12} \qquad \dfrac{1}{3} \qquad \dfrac{2}{3} \qquad \dfrac{5}{6}$

- ○ C. $\dfrac{5}{6} \qquad \dfrac{2}{3} \qquad \dfrac{1}{3} \qquad \dfrac{1}{12}$

- ○ D. $\dfrac{2}{3} \qquad \dfrac{1}{3} \qquad \dfrac{5}{6} \qquad \dfrac{1}{12}$

21. One board measures 3 feet in length by 6 inches in width.

   Which piece of wood below would have this same ratio of length to width?

   ○ A. 5 ft. to 8 in.
   ○ B. 3 in. to 6 ft.
   ○ C. 2 yd. to 1 ft.
   ○ D. 1 ft. to 2 yd.

22. If Sue pays $1.59 for a pound of lunch meat, how much will she pay for three pounds?

   Which expression is the correct ratio for this problem?

   ○ A. $1 : \$1.59 :: 3 : n$
   ○ B. $n = 3(\$1.59)$
   ○ C. $3 \times \$1.59 = n$
   ○ D. $1 \times \$1.59 \times 3 = n$

Use the illustration of the arrows to answer question 23.

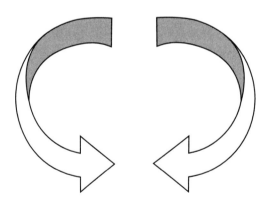

23. The arrows in the illustration are an example of which kind of transformation?

    ○ A. translation
    ○ B. stretching
    ○ C. reflection
    ○ D. rotation

Use the picture to answer question 24.

24. The school librarian rearranged a box containing biographies yesterday. She moved the box from point A to point B.

Which geometric term best describes the box's change in position?

    ○ A. refraction
    ○ B. reflection
    ○ C. translation
    ○ D. recession

Use the chart titled "Common Objects" to answer questions 25 and 26.

Common Objects

25. Which two items represent three-dimensional figures of a sphere?

    ○ A. glass, can of soup
    ○ B. megaphone, sugar cone
    ○ C. basketball, beach ball
    ○ D. cereal box, toy box

26. Which two items represent three-dimensional figures of a rectangular prism?

    ○ A. glass, can of soup
    ○ B. megaphone, sugar cone
    ○ C. basketball, beach ball
    ○ D. cereal box, toy box

27. Five televisions were purchased for a day care center. Each television cost $112.00.

    Which of the following solutions correctly uses the distributive property to find the total cost?

    ○ A. (5 x $100) + (5 x $12) = ($500 + $60) = $560.00
    ○ B. 5 + ($100 x $12) = $12,005.00
    ○ C. 5 ($100 + $12) = $500 + $20 = $620.00
    ○ D. $12 ($100 + 5) = $1,260.00

28. Correctly solve this equation using the distributive property:

    $2,010 \times 6 = n$

    ○ A. 6 (2,000 + 10) = 12,000 + 60 = 12,000
    ○ B. (2,000 x 6) + (10 x 6) = 12,000 + 60 = 12,060
    ○ C. 6 + (2,000 x 10) = 20,000 + 6 = 20,006
    ○ D. 10 (2,000 + 6) = 20,000 + 60 = 20,060

29. Use the order of operations correctly to solve this equation.

    $(4 \times 6) \times (3 + 2) - (\frac{12}{4}) = n$

    ○ A. $n = 51$
    ○ B. $n = 120$
    ○ C. $n = 117$
    ○ D. $n = 141$

30. Use the order of operations correctly to solve this equation.

    $8 + 8 \times 4 - 7 = n$

    ○ A. $n = 57$
    ○ B. $n = 33$
    ○ C. $n = 64$
    ○ D. $n = 40$

31. If (*n*) equals any even number, what equation would be used to express an odd number (*b*)?

      A. $b = n \times 1$

      B. $b = \dfrac{2}{n}$

      C. $b = n + 1$

      D. $b = n - 0$

32. If David buys two of the same CD for $26.00, how much does each CD cost?

Which equation is the correct one to use to find the solution?

      A. $\$26.00 = 2n$

      B. $\$26.00 = 2 + n$

      C. $\$26.00 = \dfrac{n}{1}$

      D. $\$26.00 = 2 - n$

33. There are three attached condos facing the riverfront. The three condos measure 60 ft. wide by 16 ft. tall; 90 ft. wide by 25 ft. tall; and 80 ft. wide by 16 ft. tall.

How much of the riverfront do these three condos occupy?

      A. 560 ft.
      B. 600 ft.
      C. 230 ft.
      D. 57 ft.

34. What is the area of a circular flower garden that surrounds the school flagpole, if the distance from the flagpole in the center to the outside wall of the flower garden is 5 ft.? ($A = \pi r^2$)

      A. 15.7 sq. ft.
      B. 78.5 sq. ft.
      C. 785 sq. ft.
      D. 157 sq. ft.

35. Kim is on the middle school track team. She is practicing for the city track meet in two weeks.

   How many kilometers can Kim walk in two hours? Choose the most reasonable measure from the choices given to answer the question.

   ○ A. 0.6 km.
   ○ B. 6 km.
   ○ C. 60 km.
   ○ D. 600 km.

36. What would be the approximate height of a telephone pole?

   ○ A. 12 cm.
   ○ B. 12 m.
   ○ C. 12 km.
   ○ D. 12 ml.

37. On the line below, construct an acute angle that measures 45°.

_____

38. On the line below, construct an obtuse angle that measures 120°.

_____

39. Estimate the product of 62 and 59.

   ○ A. 120
   ○ B. 1,200
   ○ C. 360
   ○ D. 3,600

40. Find the combined weight of three cheerleaders on the top of a pyramid formation. Sherri weighs 98 pounds, Jane weighs 102 pounds, and Cheryl weighs 111 pounds. Use front-end estimation to find the combined weight of the cheerleaders.

- ○ A. $100 + 100 + 100 + 13 = n$
- ○ B. $90 + 100 + 110 + 15 = n$
- ○ C. $90 + 100 + 100 = n$
- ○ D. $100 + 100 + 110 + 9 = n$

41. After Tiara's party she had these amounts of leftover pizza: $\frac{1}{4}$ of a sausage pizza, $\frac{5}{8}$ of a veggie pizza, $\frac{1}{2}$ of a pepperoni pizza, $\frac{3}{8}$ of a cheese pizza, and $\frac{1}{8}$ of a deluxe pizza.

Estimate how much pizza was left over?

- ○ A. $2 \frac{1}{4}$
- ○ B. 2
- ○ C. 3
- ○ D. $\frac{8}{15}$

Use the chart titled "Laura's School Books" to answer question 42.

Laura's School Books

Type of Book	Cost
History	$43.25
Math	$38.50
Science	$27.75
English	$25.75

42. Rounding to the nearest whole number, which expression best estimates the cost of Laura's books?

○ A. $43.00 + $39.00 + $28.00 + $26.00 = n
○ B. $43.00 + $38.00 + $27.00 + $25.00 = n
○ C. $44.00 + $39.00 + $28.00 + $26.00 = n
○ D. $40.00 + $40.00 + $30.00 + $30.00 = n

A survey of 20 students' favorite snacks was taken at Pike School. Use the information gathered during the survey to answer questions 43 and 44.

Sandy	– pizza	Keisha	– chips	Jeremy	– chips	David	– fruit
John	– chips	Tom	– pizza	Kevin	– candy	Angela	– pizza
Brenda	– candy	Khanh	– fruit	Tammy	– fruit	Jim	– pizza
Jon	– chips	Carol	– pizza	Vong	– fruit	Lisa	– fruit
Jane	– pizza	Laura	– candy	Danny	– pizza	Chris	– chips

43. Create a tally chart in the box to display the results of the survey.

44. Using the information from the survey, make a bar graph that displays this information.

Use the chart titled "Sales Profits Per Quarter" to answer questions 45 and 46.

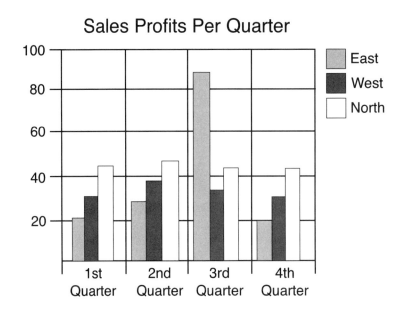

45. Read and interpret the chart titled "Sales Profits Per Quarter."

During which sales quarter were the most profits made in the East?

O A. 1st quarter
O B. 2nd quarter
O C. 3rd quarter
O D. 4th quarter

46. Based on the chart, "Sales Profits Per Quarter," which section of the country had the most consistent profits throughout the year?

O A. East
O B. West
O C. North
O D. South

Use Ryan's history grades to answer questions 47 and 48.

> Ryan's history grades for this grading period are:
> 85, 88, 92, 95, 100, 76, 84, 88, 70, 92, 88, 100, 97, 86, 88, and 90.

47. Find the average (mean) grade Ryan will have for this grading period rounded to the nearest whole number.

O A. 88.6875
O B. 89
O C. 88.7
O D. 88

48. Find the mode of Ryan's scores.

    ○ A. 100
    ○ B. 72
    ○ C. 88
    ○ D. 89

49. There are 20 candies in a bag. There are 5 red, 4 yellow, 3 brown, 3 green, 3 orange, and 2 blue.

    If Candace selects one candy from the bag, what is the probability that it will be a red one?

    ○ A. 5

    ○ B. $\dfrac{1}{5}$

    ○ C. $\dfrac{5}{20}$

    ○ D. 20%

Use the illustration of a spinner to answer question 50.

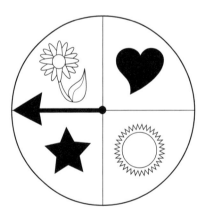

50. What is the probability (P) of the spinner stopping on a flower? Express the probability as a percentage.

    ○ A. P = 100%
    ○ B. P = 10%
    ○ C. P = 50%
    ○ D. P = 25%

End of Mathematics Test 1

Mathematics

Test 2

1. Shirley is making a quilt. On Tuesday, the square quilt measured 9 sq. ft. Throughout the week, Shirley continued to work on her quilt. By Sunday, the area of Shirley's quilt was four times larger than it was on Tuesday.

   How long would each side of Shirley's quilt be on Sunday?

   ○ A. 9 ft.
   ○ B. 6 ft.
   ○ C. 3 ft.
   ○ D. 4 ft.

2. Mrs. Gainer takes 10 points off for any late assignment.

   If Vicky receives 99 points for a report that was handed in late, what equation states the best way to find her original score?

   ○ A. 99 - 10 = 89
   ○ B. 109 - 10 = 89
   ○ C. 99 + 10 = 109
   ○ D. 99 x 10 = 990

3. Choose the sequence of numbers that would complete the table to make the following equation true.

   $3n + 2 = x$

n	0	1	2	___	5	___
x	2	5	___	11	___	23

   ○ A. 8, 3, 17, 7
   ○ B. 6, 3, 13, 6
   ○ C. 7, 3, 16, 8
   ○ D. 8, 3, 16, 6

Use the chart titled "Relay Team Results" to answer question 4.

Relay Team Results

Runner	Time in Seconds
Tammy	18.1
Rose	17.5
Leah	19.6
Jean	16.8

4. Which equation shows the total time for the relay team?

   ○ A. 18.1 + 17.5 + 19.6 + 16.8 ÷ 4 = 18 seconds
   ○ B. 18.1 + 17.5 + 19.6 + 16.8 x 4 = 288 seconds
   ○ C. 18.1 + 17.5 + 19.6 + 16.8 - 4 = 68 seconds
   ○ D. 18.1 + 17.5 + 19.6 + 16.8 = 72 seconds

5. Four boys decide to order pizza Friday night. The boys plan to share two pizzas. They have a coupon for two pizzas for $8.99.

   If there are eight slices in each pizza, how much will each slice of pizza cost?

   ○ A. more than $0.50 a slice
   ○ B. less than $0.50 a slice
   ○ C. not enough information
   ○ D. exactly $0.50 a slice

6. In a book on snails, there is an average of 11 words in a line of print.

   If one page has 34 lines of print, estimate how many words would be on that page.

   ○ A. 384
   ○ B. 320
   ○ C. 350
   ○ D. 3,374

7. Which words correctly complete the number sentence?

   409.653 _____ 4096.53

   ○ A. is equal to
   ○ B. is greater than
   ○ C. is less than
   ○ D. is greater than or equal to

Use the chart titled "Band Boosters' Refreshments" to answer question 8.

Band Boosters' Refreshments

Hot Dogs	Soda	Chips	Candy	Coffee	Gum
$1.00	$0.50	$0.50	$0.50	$0.50	$0.05

8. Band Boosters sell refreshments for the prices listed in the table titled "Band Boosters' Refreshments."

   Sean ordered a hot dog, a soda, and 6 pieces of gum. Sean's friend Jamal placed the exact same order.

   If Sean paid for his order and Jamal's order, how much did Sean spend?

   ○ A. $1.55
   ○ B. $1.80
   ○ C. $3.10
   ○ D. $3.60

9. Sandy ate one-fourth of a pizza.

   If one-fourth of the pizza equals two pieces, how many pieces were in the pizza?

   ○ A. 4 pieces
   ○ B. 6 pieces
   ○ C. 8 pieces
   ○ D. 10 pieces

10. A recipe for nachos uses three-fourths of a pound of cheese.

   If you plan to double the recipe, how much cheese will you need?

   ○ A. $\dfrac{3}{4}$ pound

   ○ B. $\dfrac{6}{8}$ pound

   ○ C. $1\dfrac{3}{4}$ pounds

   ○ D. $1\dfrac{1}{2}$ pounds

11. Jamie has $24.00 to spend at the mall. She spends one-fourth of her money on food.

   How much money did Jamie spend on food?

   ○ A. $6.00
   ○ B. $8.00
   ○ C. $10.00
   ○ D. $12.00

12. Phil's quiz grades are 21, 20, 23, and 22. Keisha's quiz grades are 22, 18, 21, and 24. Tori's quiz grades are 19, 24, 17, and 23. Their teacher said they all have a rounded average of 21 points.

Which student has the highest exact average?

○ A. Phil
○ B. Keisha
○ C. Tori
○ D. All three students have the same exact average.

13. The selling price of a duffel bag is calculated by adding $10.50 to the dealer cost.

If the bag costs the dealer $8.32, what will the selling price be?

○ A. $18.50
○ B. $18.82
○ C. $18.92
○ D. $18.99

14. Vong's mother spent $1.68 on grapes, $2.32 on apples, $2.12 on oranges, and $1.37 on bananas.

How much did she spend on fruit?

○ A. $6.12
○ B. $7.42
○ C. $7.49
○ D. $8.49

15. Jasmina's cookie recipe calls for $\frac{1}{2}$ cup of sugar. Merima's recipe calls for $\frac{3}{4}$ cup of sugar.

If they both doubled their recipes to make more cookies, who would use more sugar?

○ A. Jasmina
○ B. Merima
○ C. Both recipes use the same amount of sugar.
○ D. There is not enough information to solve this problem.

16. Jim uses a five gallon bucket to fill aquariums.

   If he gives each aquarium two gallons of water, how many aquariums can he fill with one full bucket?

   ○ A. $\dfrac{2}{5}$

   ○ B. $\dfrac{4}{5}$

   ○ C. $1\dfrac{1}{2}$

   ○ D. $2\dfrac{1}{2}$

17. Place these numbers in order from least to greatest value.

   2.10, 0.21, 21.0, 2.01

   ○ A. 2.01, 2.10, 0.21, 21.0
   ○ B. 0.21, 2.01, 2.10, 21.0
   ○ C. 21.0, 2.10, 2.01, 0.21
   ○ D. 2.10, 2.01, 21.0, 0.21

18. What fractional part of $1,000.00 is $20.00?

   ○ A. $\dfrac{1}{5}$

   ○ B. $\dfrac{1}{10}$

   ○ C. $\dfrac{1}{50}$

   ○ D. $\dfrac{1}{100}$

19. If you scored an 80% on a 20 point quiz, how many items did you miss?

    ○ A. 2 items
    ○ B. 3 items
    ○ C. 4 items
    ○ D. 5 items

20. Put these fractions in order from the least to the greatest value.

$$\frac{3}{4} \qquad \frac{1}{8} \qquad \frac{3}{16} \qquad \frac{5}{8}$$

    ○ A. $\dfrac{1}{8} \qquad \dfrac{3}{4} \qquad \dfrac{5}{8} \qquad \dfrac{3}{16}$

    ○ B. $\dfrac{3}{16} \qquad \dfrac{5}{8} \qquad \dfrac{3}{4} \qquad \dfrac{1}{8}$

    ○ C. $\dfrac{1}{8} \qquad \dfrac{5}{8} \qquad \dfrac{3}{4} \qquad \dfrac{3}{16}$

    ○ D. $\dfrac{1}{8} \qquad \dfrac{3}{16} \qquad \dfrac{5}{8} \qquad \dfrac{3}{4}$

21. If a farmer has a 5 acre pasture and 150 cows, what is the ratio of cows per acre?

    ○ A. 10 cows per acre
    ○ B. 20 cows per acre
    ○ C. 30 cows per acre
    ○ D. 50 cows per acre

Use the illustration of parallelograms to answer question 22.

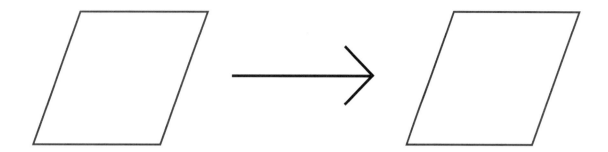

22. Decide which name best identifies this kind of transformation.

   ○ A. rotation
   ○ B. translation
   ○ C. reflection
   ○ D. transformation

23. Draw a reflection of the arrow in the box on the right.

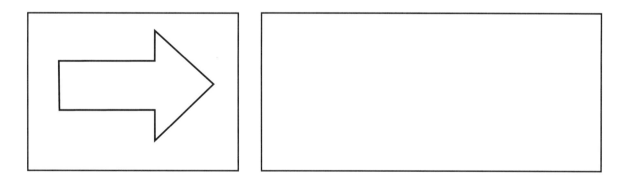

24. If Kathy makes $25.00 in four hours, how much will she make in two eight-hour days?

   ○ A. $32.00
   ○ B. $50.00
   ○ C. $82.00
   ○ D. $100.00

Use the illustration below to answer question 25.

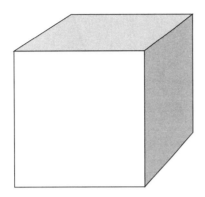

25. What is this three-dimensional figure?

    ○ A. a cylinder
    ○ B. a sphere
    ○ C. a cube
    ○ D. a square

26. Which name correctly identifies the three-dimensional shape of most cans of fruits, soups, and vegetables?

    ○ A. cylinder
    ○ B. round
    ○ C. sphere
    ○ D. circle

27. Lonnie knows she has to collect $2.05 from 9 students. She uses the distributive property to figure out the total amount of money she will collect.

Which solution below shows the correct process?

    ○ A. ($2.00 x 9) + ($0.05 x 9) = ($18.00) + ($0.45) = $18.45
    ○ B. 9($2.05) = $18.45
    ○ C. $2.05 x 9 = $18.45
    ○ D. 9 + $2.05 = $11.05

28. Jada's school supplies were $21.75. She has $8.25 left.

Which equation correctly expresses the amount of money Jada had originally?

- A. $\$21.75 - \$8.25 = n$
- B. $\$21.75 + \$8.25 = n$
- C. $\$8.25 \times n = \$21.75$
- D. $\$21.75 + n = \$8.25$

29. Use the order of operations correctly to solve this equation.

$7 + 6 + 3 \times 12 - 4 = n$

- A. $n = 45$
- B. $n = 188$
- C. $n = 117$
- D. $n = 49$

30. Use the order of operations correctly to solve this equation.

$9 - 3 + 15 \times 2 + 8 = n$

- A. $n = 58$
- B. $n = 50$
- C. $n = 44$
- D. $n = 38$

31. Mrs. Zanta told her students they would get five points for every correct response (n) on the chapter quiz.

Which equation best expresses how students can calculate their grades (%)?

- A. $5 + n = \%$
- B. $5n = \%$
- C. $n + 5 = \%$
- D. $5n + 5 = \%$

32. Which equation would be used to find the area of a room that is 12 ft. by 17 ft.?

   ○ A. 12 ft. x 17 ft. = 204 sq. ft.
   ○ B. 12 ft. + 17 ft. = 29 ft.
   ○ C. 17 ft. - 12 ft. = 5 ft.
   ○ D. 12 ft. + 12 ft. + 17 ft. + 17 ft. = 58 ft.

33. The perimeter of a triangular traffic island is 70 ft.

   If two sides are equal, and they are each 23 ft. long, which equation would be used to find the length of the third side?

   ○ A. $2n(23) = 70$ ft.
   ○ B. $2n + 23 = 70$ ft.
   ○ C. $(2 \times 23) + n = 70$ ft.
   ○ D. $n + 23 = 70$ ft.

34. Students in a class measure a computer keyboard.

   Which measurement would be the closest to their exact measure?

   ○ A. 40 mm.
   ○ B. 40 cm.
   ○ C. 40 m.
   ○ D. 40 km.

35. The approximate length of a pencil would be best represented by which choice?

   ○ A. 18 cm.
   ○ B. 18 mm.
   ○ C. 18 ml.
   ○ D. 18 m.

36. The width of a house would be best represented by which choice?

    ○ A. 12 cm.
    ○ B. 12 ml.
    ○ C. 12 m.
    ○ D. 12 km.

37. What is the name of an angle that measures 63°?

    ○ A. acute
    ○ B. obtuse
    ○ C. reflex
    ○ D. oblong

38. What is the name of an angle that measures 128°?

    ○ A. acute
    ○ B. obtuse
    ○ C. reflex
    ○ D. oblong

39. Estimate the price of a new car to the nearest hundred dollars if the actual price is $21,742.67.

    ○ A. $21,743.00
    ○ B. $21,750.00
    ○ C. $21,800.00
    ○ D. $21,700.00

40. The average body temperature of humans is 98.6°. Amy's temperature is 99.3° and is considered within the 'normal' range for the human body.

If both temperatures were rounded to the nearest degree, would they be:

○ A. the same.
○ B. 1 degree different.
○ C. 2 degrees different.
○ D. 7 degrees different.

41. Choose the best estimate for the sum of these mixed numbers.

$$2 \frac{6}{7} + 5 \frac{1}{7} = n$$

○ A. $n = 6$
○ B. $n = 7$
○ C. $n = 8$
○ D. $n = 9$

42. Choose the best estimate for the sum of these mixed numbers.

$$7 \frac{1}{4} + 5 \frac{1}{7} = n$$

○ A. $n = 12$
○ B. $n = 16$
○ C. $n = 16.5$
○ D. $n = 17$

43. Construct a graph using the information in Table 1: Animal Kingdom's Monthly Sales. Remember to include all parts of a graph.

The Animal Kingdom pet shop reported gross monthly sales in amounts rounded to the nearest thousand. The monthly sales are listed in the table.

Table 1: Animal Kingdom's Monthly Sales

January	February	March	April	May	June
$15,000.00	$16,000.00	$19,000.00	$16,000.00	$16,000.00	$18,000.00

Construct graph here.

Use the bar graph titled "Sales Profits Per Quarter" to answer question 44.

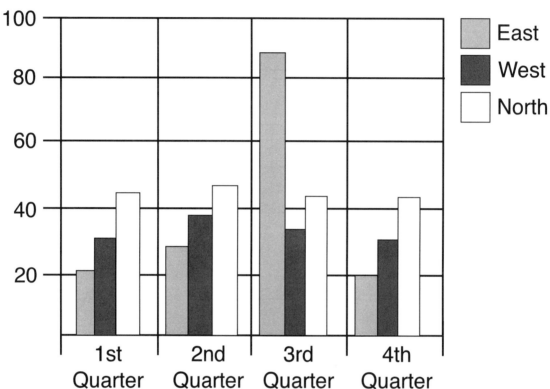

Sales Profits Per Quarter

44. Read and interpret the bar graph to find which region had the highest profits during the 3rd quarter.

   ○ A. East
   ○ B. West
   ○ C. South
   ○ D. North

Use the pie graph titled "January Expenses" to answer question 45.

January Expenses

45. Read and interpret the pie graph to determine the largest expense for this salesperson in January.

   ○ A. food
   ○ B. gas
   ○ C. motel
   ○ D. tips

46. The daily high temperatures this week were: 69°, 73°, 75°, 80°, 84°, 84°, and 89°.

   Find the mean temperature for the week. Round your response to the tenths place.

   ○ A. 78.5°
   ○ B. 79.1°
   ○ C. 79.2°
   ○ D. 80.0°

47. The daily high temperatures this week were: 69°, 73°, 80°, 84°, 84°, 89°, and 75°.

   Find the mode of the temperatures for this week expressed as a whole number.

   ○ A. 69°
   ○ B. 89°
   ○ C. 84°
   ○ D. 80°

48. The daily high temperatures this week were: 69°, 73°, 75°, 80°, 84°, 84°, and 89°.

   Find the median temperature for this week expressed as a whole number.

   ○ A. 69°
   ○ B. 89°
   ○ C. 84°
   ○ D. 80°

49. A coin has two sides: one labeled 'heads' and one labeled 'tails.'

   At a coin toss before a football game, what is the probability the coin will land on 'heads' as called by the team captain?

   ○ A. 2

   ○ B. $\dfrac{1}{2}$

   ○ C. $\dfrac{2}{1}$

   ○ D. 1

50. A coin has two sides: one labeled 'heads' and one labeled 'tails.'

   At a coin toss before a football game, what is the probability the coin will land on 'heads' as called by the team captain?

   Express the probability as a percent.

   ○ A. 20%
   ○ B. 25%
   ○ C. 40%
   ○ D. 50%

End of Mathematics Test 2

Citizenship

Test 1

Before you begin Test 1, read through the test-taking strategies for Citizenship on the next page. These strategies give you a chance to practice answering short-answer and extended-reponse items.

Test 1 questions begins on page 174.

Short-Answer Items

Read through the question below.

Until about ten years ago, relatively few people had cable TV. Now about 90% of U.S. citizens are able to watch cable TV. Most cable TV systems have certain channels dedicated to politics. Some of these channels broadcast debates, Congress in session, and speeches by politicians. Use the graph titled "Thursday's Political Programs" to find out which political cable programs are available on Thursday and the number of projected viewers for each program. If you wanted to run a commercial, on Thursday, about the importance of voting, what program would you select and why?

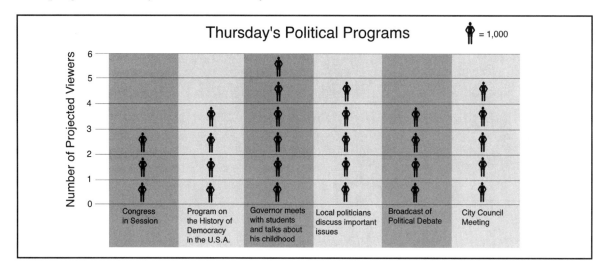

_____
_____
_____
_____
_____
_____

Look at the graph to help you make your decision about choosing a program during which to run your commercial. Because your commercial is an advertisement, you want to consider the number of projected viewers for each program. This will help you determine how many people will be watching your commercial.

The following is an example of a 2-point response:

It is best to run the commercial during the program in which the governor meets with students and talks about his childhood. The projected number of viewers is six thousand. This is the most viewers of all programs. Therefore, more people will be watching the commercial on the importance of voting.

Extended-Response Items

Read through the passage and answer the question below.

Most state and national elections are held on Tuesdays. The polls are usually open from 6:00 a.m. until 7:00 p.m. This system was created to give everyone the best possible opportunity to vote. It allows people to vote before work, after work, or anytime they feel is convenient. Also, it does not conflict with people's religious beliefs, since most religions are observed on either a Saturday or a Sunday.

However, some people argue this voting process is unfair to those who live in the western part of the United States. Because of the different times zones in our country, people in the eastern part of the country are finished voting well before people in the western states. When it is 7:00 p.m. in New York, it is only 4:00 p.m. in Los Angeles, California. Thus, people in Los Angeles have three more hours to vote. Because of TV and radio, people in the western states learn of election results in eastern states even before their polls close. When people in the western states hear what people have decided upon in the eastern part of the United States, it may change their minds about voting. People may choose not to vote because they feel the vote has already been decided.

According to this selection, why do people feel the voting process is unfair to voters in the western U.S.?

_____

_____

_____

_____

_____

_____

_____

_____

The first thing you must do is carefully read the passage. You will find that there are many facts that will help you explain your answer. Think about all of these when you jot down ideas in the margin, underline key words, and try to organize your thoughts. Read the question to yourself, and then read your answer silently to yourself. Does what you answered make sense? Did you leave out anything important, or do you want to add anything new? You may also want to use your pencil to circle important words in the question to remind you what you need to include in your answers.

The following is an example of a 4-point response:

Some people feel the voting process is unfair because those in the eastern U.S. have finished voting three hours before those in the western U.S. As a result, people living in western states learn of the results in eastern states before their own polls close. This causes some people not to vote because they feel the decision has already been made. Therefore, some people feel voters of the U.S., as a whole, are not given an equal opportunity to decide the election results.

1. The Industrial Revolution, which began around 1775, has also been called the Age of Machines. It was during this time that the steam engine was created. This invention enabled more powerful machines to be used in the mining of coal and other minerals. It was also used to manufacture goods faster and more inexpensively.

   Which of the following events occurred during the period of the Industrial Revolution?

   ○ A. People made spearheads by chipping away a piece of flint with a stone.
   ○ B. Robert Fulton developed the first steamboat, which many people called "Fulton's Folly."
   ○ C. For the first time, a person walked on the moon.
   ○ D. Christopher Columbus arrived in the New World. He traveled with three ships: the Nina, the Pinta, and the Santa Maria.

Use the time line titled "North America and Europe from 1900 to 1920" to answer question 2.

North America and Europe from 1900 to 1920

North America		Europe
Coca Cola introduced	-1900-	Germany increases sea power
Teddy Roosevelt elected President		
		Women's Union formed in Britain
	-1905-	
San Francisco earthquake		
First comic strips appear		
		First steel and glass building built
Perry reaches North Pole		
	-1910-	
Mexican dictator Diaz overthrown		Amundsen reaches South Pole
U.S. troops occupy Nicaragua		Titanic sinks
Panama Canal opens		World War I begins
	-1915-	Italy joins Allies
		Irish revolt against British Rule
U.S. enters World War I		Russian Revolution begins
		World War I ends
Women granted right to vote in U.S.	-1920-	Red Army wins Russian Civil War

2. Based on the time line, which of the following statements is true?

   ○ A. The United States entered World War I the same year the Russian Revolution began.
   ○ B. Amundsen reached the South Pole before Perry reached the North Pole.
   ○ C. The Panama Canal opened the year after World War I began.
   ○ D. The sinking of the Titanic caused Teddy Roosevelt to be elected President of the United States.

3. Washington, D.C., has not always been the capital of the United States. The first U.S. capital was Philadelphia, Pennsylvania. From there it was moved to Baltimore, Maryland; New York City, New York; Trenton, New Jersey; and Princeton, New Jersey. Each year tourists from all over the world travel to the capital of the United States without knowing it has not been the only U.S. capital.

   What is the main idea of the reading selection?

   ○ A. Each year tourists from all over the world travel to Washington, D.C.
   ○ B. Washington, D.C., was the first capital of the United States.
   ○ C. The United States has had several capitals.
   ○ D. Princeton, New Jersey, was once the capital of the United States.

4. On May 4, 1970, National Guardsmen shot and killed four students and wounded several others at Kent State University in Kent, Ohio. The shootings occurred during a student protest against U.S. involvement in the Vietnam War. Following the shootings, reporters questioned many people. Among the people questioned were a student who heard about the shootings after she left class, a professor of one of the wounded students, the president of the university, and a student who was standing beside one of the students who was hit during the shootings.

   In relating the actual events of the shootings, who is the most reliable of the people questioned?

   Explain your answer.

   _____

   _____

   _____

5. Who would be the most reliable source related to the events that occurred during a bank robbery?

    ○ A. The teller at the bank who was the victim of the gunman in the holdup.
    ○ B. The president of the bank who heard about the robbery from his employees.
    ○ C. The wife of the bank teller who was robbed.
    ○ D. The reporter who submitted the article to the local newspaper.

6. George Washington Carver was born into slavery in Missouri in 1861, but he became free at the end of the Civil War. After being orphaned, he was raised by his former owners. He worked as a cook through college. After earning his master's degree, Carver became the head of the Department of Agriculture at the Tuskegee Institute in Alabama. He experimented and found that peanuts grow well in the South and improve the soil. He developed crop rotation, a method of farming in which different crops are planted in a field each year to enrich the soil. Carver also developed over 325 different uses for peanuts, including food substitutes, dyes, and soaps. These two developments have changed the way Americans farm and eat.

    What two achievements of George Washington Carver affected the way in which American people live today?

    _____

    _____

7. Helen Keller was born June 27, 1880, in Alabama. When she was 19 months old, Helen became ill with a fever that caused her to become deaf and blind. Because she could not hear the sounds, Helen could not speak. Her teacher, Anne Sullivan, taught Helen to read Braille and to write using a special typewriter. Helen went on to graduate with honors from Radcliffe College, one of the nation's most famous colleges for women. After graduation, Helen spent her life helping the handicapped. Largely because of her efforts, people came to realize that handicapped people could be educated and could live very productive lives.

    Helen Keller became very famous because of her contribution to the American way of life.

    Which of the following is Helen's contribution?

    ○ A. She was born in Alabama in 1880.
    ○ B. She had a fever when she was 19 months old.
    ○ C. She could not speak.
    ○ D. She made people realize that handicapped people could be educated and could live very productive lives.

8. In 1854, Charles Loring Brace, a Methodist minister and founder of the Children's Aid Society of New York, realized there were far more orphans than he could find homes for in New York. As many as one thousand children were abandoned each year at New York's Foundling Hospital. Many other children were living on the streets and stealing food and clothing in order to stay alive. Loring felt the orphans would live better lives away from the crowds and crime in the city. He began, with the help of area businessmen, to send these children to the West, where he felt they would have wholesome family lives on farms. The children were put on trains that traveled to several of the western states. At each stop, the children were paraded before the townspeople, who could select those they wanted to adopt.

By the time these orphan trains stopped running in 1959, approximately 350,000 children had been transported to the West. Loring's orphan trains were important in the development of the United States. They helped to populate the West, and they provided orphaned and abandoned children with wholesome family lives, which they would not have had otherwise.

Explain how Charles Loring Brace contributed to the cultural development of the United States.

_____

_____

_____

_____

9. Joan of Arc was born in France around 1412. Raised as a peasant, she claimed she heard the voices of Saint Catherine, Saint Michael, and Saint Margaret telling her to free France from the control of the English. In 1429, to begin her quest to free France, she began to travel with the future King Charles VII, who had been denied the throne by the English. Charles placed Joan in command of his troops, and she led an attack on the city of Orleans. Joan went on to Compiegne, where she was captured and sold to the British. The English turned her over to a church court, which found her guilty of witchcraft. She was burned at the stake on May 30, 1431.

Which of the following caused Joan of Arc to join the battle to free France from the British?

- ○ A. She wanted to be queen of France.
- ○ B. She was in love with King Charles.
- ○ C. She believed she heard the voices of saints telling her to free France.
- ○ D. She had been raised as a peasant.

10. Henry VIII, king of England from 1509 to 1547, wanted a male heir. When his wife, Catherine of Aragon, gave birth to a girl, Henry asked the Catholic Church to grant him a divorce. The Church refused the divorce, and Henry had his Parliament pass a law giving power in matters of marriage to the archbishop of Canterbury. The archbishop of Canterbury granted Henry his divorce. The Pope then stated the king and the entire country of England could no longer belong to the Catholic Church. Henry declared himself supreme head of the church in England, and all of the payments normally made to the Pope now went to the crown. It was treason to question either Henry's new title or the succession. In 1534, the English government confiscated the belongings of the Catholic Church. Protestants credited him with initiating the Protestant Reformation.

Which of the following caused King Henry VIII of England to ask for a divorce?

○ A. His mother did not like his wife.
○ B. He wanted a male heir.
○ C. He did not like the Catholic Church.
○ D. He wanted more money.

11. Michelangelo Buonarroti, who lived from 1475 to 1564, was an Italian painter, sculptor, architect, and poet. As a boy, Michelangelo preferred to draw rather than study. Later, from 1490 to 1492, Michelangelo lived in the house of Lorenzo de' Medici, a wealthy citizen of Florence, Italy. Medici helped artists, philosophers, and poets financially, and many of them gathered at the Medici home. The presence of these artists, philosophers, and poets, as well as the examples of classical art that Medici collected, affected both Michelangelo's beliefs and his art. This helped him to become one of the most famous artists in history. His outstanding works include the ceiling of the Sistine Chapel and the sculptures of the Pietà and David.

What was an event that greatly influenced Michelangelo and helped him to develop into one of the greatest artists of all time?

_____

_____

_____

12. A series of laws and policies made discrimination against blacks legal in South Africa. This legal discrimination is called apartheid. It forced the black population to live on small sections of infertile land called "homelands." Residents of the homelands were required to carry "pass books" with their fingerprints, photographs, and information related to any travel to non-black areas. Overpopulation of the blacks occurred in these areas. In addition, eighty percent of the black population lived in poverty. Because there were few job opportunities, blacks often had to travel hundreds of miles on overcrowded buses to find work.

The end of apartheid has given the blacks of South Africa hope for the future.

Which of the following will change because of the end of apartheid?

- ○ A. The blacks will have to live in segregated areas called "homelands."
- ○ B. The blacks will be able to own land in areas outside of the "homelands."
- ○ C. The blacks will have fewer job opportunities.
- ○ D. The whites will have to become farmers.

13. The Taliban, a military group that controls parts of the country of Afghanistan, has enforced rules related to women. Under their rule, most women are forbidden to work outside the home, attend school, or leave their homes unless accompanied by a male. Women are required to completely cover their bodies with clothing that leaves only a small opening for them to be able to see. Windows of women's homes must be painted black. Women who break these laws are beaten or killed.

Before the Taliban gained power in Afghanistan, approximately half of the university students, teachers, government workers, and doctors were women. At that time, women were permitted to move freely throughout society, similar to the freedom women of the United States enjoy today.

State two differences in the treatment of the women of Afghanistan before the rule of the Taliban and after the Taliban came into power.

_____

_____

_____

_____

14. In 1847, "Indian Jim" took James Marshall to the Maidu village in California, 45 miles northeast of Sacramento. Marshall decided to build a sawmill there. It was on this land that gold was discovered. Marshall was given credit, but others think "Indian Jim" found the gold while digging a channel to provide power for the sawmill.

During the first few months following the discovery, Native Americans and white people both panned for gold. Four thousand Native Americans were employed in gold fields compared to 2,000 whites. The Native Americans even invented a device called "Long Tom" or the "sluice box," which was used for catching gold pieces.

In 1850, people from all over the country began flocking to the Maidu village in California to look for gold. As a result, the Native Americans were treated poorly and eventually driven out of California because of accusations stating they were not peaceful.

What was one of the reasons the people in California drove the Native Americans out of California?

_____

_____

_____

15. During the potato famine in Ireland in the mid-1800s, many Irish immigrated to the United States. Unfortunately, upon arriving in this country, they found discrimination. Many people believed the Irish were lazy, dishonest, violent, and heavy drinkers. Because of these beliefs, many employers did not want to hire them.

Which of the following statements can be inferred from reading the selection?

○ A. The Irish had difficulty earning a living because they could not find jobs.
○ B. The Irish decided to go back to Ireland.
○ C. The Native Americans and the Irish became good friends.
○ D. The Irish became very rich when they arrived in this country.

16. Dutch and English colonists brought the first quilts to America. These first quilts were appliquéd. This meant the quilts contained pieces of fabric that were cut out and sewn into pictures on the base fabric. Fabric was often expensive and hard to get, so women would cut geometric shapes from scraps of fabric and piece them together to form the top of the quilt. These types of quilts were called "patchwork quilts." In the years before the Civil War, African-American women would sew patchwork quilts that gave messages to the runaway slaves who were trying to find their way north to freedom. Because it was illegal for slaves to learn to read or write, the placement of the geometric shapes on the quilt gave the message. The quilts were then hung out on a fence to dry or "air out." This allowed a method of communication that was invisible to slave holders. Quilts continue to be found in American homes today.

Which of the following groups contributed to the American culture by bringing quilts to this country?

○　A.　Japanese immigrants
○　B.　African-American slaves
○　C.　French immigrants
○　D.　English and Dutch colonists

17. As immigrants from various countries around the world came to the United States, they introduced foods they had known and loved in their homelands. Italians have been no exception to this rule. In addition to contributions in music, theater, and the arts, they brought foods such as pizza, broccoli, spaghetti, and hearty red wines. Today, we find these foods in our restaurants, our grocery stores, and our homes.

According to this selection, what was one of the greatest influences Italians have had on the culture of the United States?

_____

_____

_____

Use the map titled "Map of the World" to answer questions 18 and 19.

Map of the World

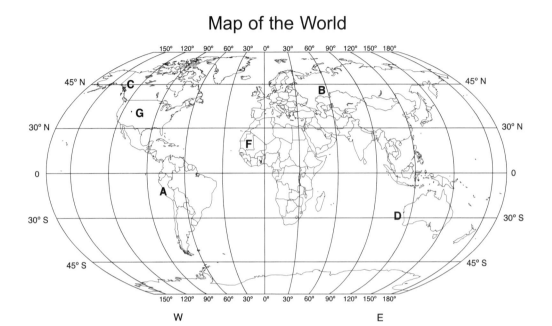

18. The city of Sitka is located at 45° N and 135° W.

    Which of the following letters shows the location of Sitka on the map?

    ○ A. letter B
    ○ B. letter D
    ○ C. letter A
    ○ D. letter C

19. Which of the following letters shows the location of 43° N and 50° E on the map?

    ○ A. letter B
    ○ B. letter F
    ○ C. letter G
    ○ D. letter C

Use the map titled "Land Use in the United States" for question 20.

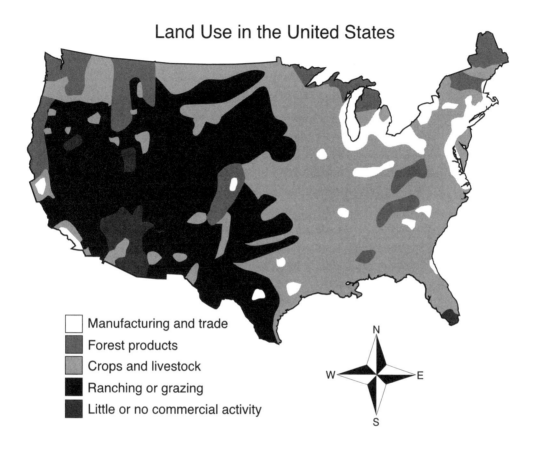

Land Use in the United States

Manufacturing and trade
Forest products
Crops and livestock
Ranching or grazing
Little or no commercial activity

20. Which part of the map would you use to find where manufacturing and trade are major sources of land use?

○ A. the title of the map
○ B. the compass rose
○ C. the key or legend
○ D. the outline of the country

Use the map titled "Time Zones of the Continental United States" to answer questions 21 and 22.

Time Zones of the Continental United States

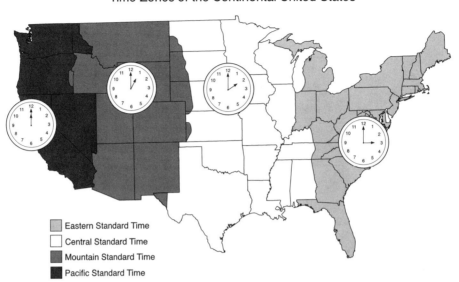

Eastern Standard Time
Central Standard Time
Mountain Standard Time
Pacific Standard Time

21. Tommy Walker lives in the Mountain Standard time zone. When installing his new computer program, he realizes he needs to speak with a technician for help. The customer support office of the computer software company, located in the Pacific Standard time zone, closes each day at 7:00 p.m. Pacific Standard time.

If it is 5:30 p.m. on Tommy's clock, will he be able to speak with a customer service representative?

Explain how you arrived at your answer.

_____

_____

22. Justin Burning was traveling from his home in Peoria, Arizona, located in the Mountain Standard time zone, to the home of his friend, Rick Nay. Rick lived in the Eastern Standard time zone.

If the flight left at 8:00 a.m., and took three hours, at what time would the plane arrive at the airport near Rick's house?

○ A. 7:00 a.m.
○ B. 8:00 a.m.
○ C. noon
○ D. 1:00 p.m.

184   © 2000 Englefield and Arnold, Inc.

Use the two maps titled "Climates of Australia" and "Major Cities of Australia" to answer question 23.

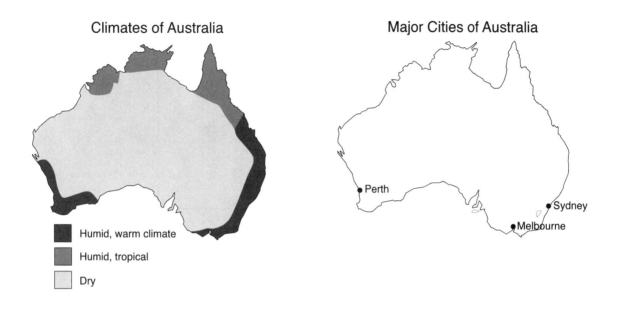

Climates of Australia

■ Humid, warm climate
▨ Humid, tropical
□ Dry

Major Cities of Australia

● Perth
● Sydney
● Melbourne

23. After studying the two maps, explain why the three major cities of Australia were established in their present locations.

_____

_____

_____

_____

_____

Use the map titled "Southwestern Europe" to answer question 24.

Southwestern Europe

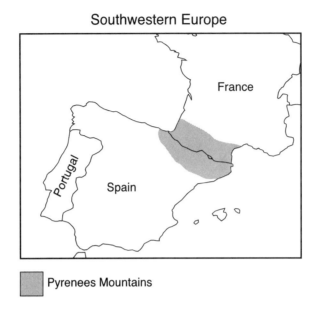

Pyrenees Mountains

24. France and Spain are both located in southwestern Europe, but they are different in language and culture.

   After studying the map of southwestern Europe, explain why the languages and cultures of Spain and France are different.

   _____

   _____

   _____

   _____

Use the map titled "North Carolina" to answer question 25.

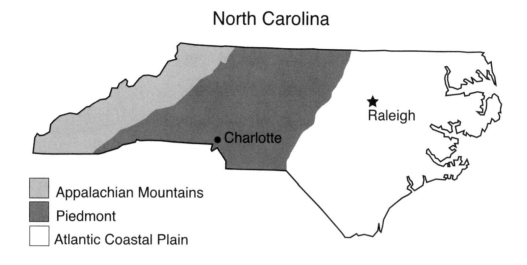

North Carolina

Appalachian Mountains
Piedmont
Atlantic Coastal Plain

25. Of the three main physical regions of North Carolina, which one does not have a major city?

_____

_____

26. Rome, the capital of Italy and a major city of Europe, is the home of many famous buildings, monuments, and works of art. The buildings include the Pantheon, an ancient Roman temple, and the Colosseum, a huge outdoor theater that held as many as 50,000 people. There are also many beautiful and historic churches and palaces. The Basilica of Saint Peter in Chains, contains a sculpture of Moses created by Renaissance artist Michelangelo. A bronze statue of Emperor Marcus Aurelius, the Trevi Fountain, and the famous Spanish Steps are all located in Rome. Tourists from all over the world travel to this city to see these historical and artistic treasures.

According to the selection above, which of the following is the reason that people from all parts of the world travel to Rome?

○ A. politics
○ B. religion
○ C. communism
○ D. tourism

27. New York City is home of both the New York Stock Exchange and the American Stock Exchange, the two largest exchanges in the world. The headquarters of many national and international corporations are located in New York City. At New York City's World Trade Center, natural resources, crops, and manufactured goods are exchanged.

People from various countries generally have contact with one another because of trade, politics, religion, or tourism.

Based on the reading selection, what is one reason for contact between New York City and the rest of the world?

_____

28. Both natural and synthetic rubber, chemicals such as carbon black oils, waxes, and fabric are used in the manufacturing of tires.

Natural rubber is an example of which of the following factors of production?

    O   A. land
    O   B. labor
    O   C. capital
    O   D. entrepreneurship

29. Petroleum is an example of the "land" factor of production. It is used for providing us with gasoline to power our cars and trucks.

List one alternative use for the petroleum.

_____

30. A doctor in a retirement community realized the residents of the town were in need of increasing quantities of medical supplies. Unfortunately for the senior citizens, the closest medical supply company was located in a neighboring town. The doctor decided to sell medical supplies at his office.

What factor influenced the doctor's decision to sell medical supplies?

    O   A. holiday and seasonal needs
    O   B. demand
    O   C. too much competition
    O   D. changes in the cost of materials

31. Beth Beha had to shop for hot dogs, buns, and potato chips for her son Patrick's baseball picnic. At the store, she discovered the Best Baked brand buns were 10 cents more per package than the generic buns. The Crispy Crunchy brand potato chips were 50 cents more per package than the generic brand potato chips. Beth decided to buy the generic brand of both items.

Which of the following factors influenced her decision to purchase the generic brand items?

○ A. price
○ B. advertising
○ C. quality
○ D. packaging

32. Chris Thompson was trying to decide what to buy his mother for her birthday. He saw a sale ad for a Beauticare brand hair drier. Chris knew his mother's drier had recently stopped working, and he decided to buy the Beauticare brand hair drier and give it to her.

Name two factors that influenced Rick's decision to purchase the Beauticare brand hair drier.

_____

_____

33. Families showing their love and appreciation of their mothers and grandmothers have made Mother's Day the biggest flower-giving day of the year. In addition, many people are shopping for seasonal plants for their gardens or hanging baskets to put on their porches and patios. Florists work from sunrise to sunset in the days before this holiday in order to meet the demand.

Explain what effect the high demand for flowers and plants on Mother's Day could have on the price of plants at that time of year.

_____

_____

_____

34. A company that owned a chain of large bookstores built a new bookstore across the street from a very small children's bookstore. After a short period of time, the owner of the small bookstore was forced to close her store. The closing of the small bookstore is an example of a disadvantage of competition in the marketplace.

    Explain what caused the owner of the small bookstore to close her store.

    _____

    _____

    _____

    _____

35. Japan does not have many of the minerals it needs, such as iron ore, copper, tin, lead, coal, yet it is known world-wide for manufacturing electronics. Some of the products it exports are cameras, video recorders, radios, televisions, and tape recorders.

    The United States is rich in many minerals, yet most of the manufacturing of electronics is no longer done in this country. The United States imports vast quantities of electronic goods.

    Based upon the reading selection, explain the potential trade relationship between Japan and the United States.

    _____

    _____

    _____

    _____

36. Australia is a member of the World Trade Organization. For years, Australia has traded with countries such as Japan, South Korea, and New Zealand. However, new markets are being developed in Asia.

   Malaysia, a country in Asia, produces large amounts of office equipment, but needs to import food from other countries. Australia produces large amounts of cereals, but needs office equipment.

   Which of the following is a probable trade relationship between Australia and Malaysia?

   ○ A. Australia will buy cereals from Malaysia, and Malaysia will buy office equipment from Australia.
   ○ B. Malaysia will buy cereals from Australia, and Australia will buy office equipment from Malaysia.
   ○ C. Malaysia will sell office equipment to the Americans and the British.
   ○ D. There will be no trade relations between the two countries.

37. What is the main function of the executive branch of government?

   _____

   _____

38. Which of the following is an activity carried out by the legislative branch of government?

   ○ A. writing proposed legislation and holding committee hearings
   ○ B. appointing officials and coordinating work of agencies
   ○ C. conducting trials
   ○ D. sentencing convicted persons

39. Parents of children in a neighborhood elementary school were very angry about overcrowding within the school. Tutors and parent volunteers had to work with children in the hallways because of lack of space. The overcrowding was so severe that all of the kindergarten classes and two of the second grade classes had to share classrooms. Parents attended the meeting of the Board of Education and wrote letters to City Council requesting a solution to the problem. The parents' actions are an example of democracy in action.

What is one characteristic of democracy demonstrated by these actions?

_____

_____

40. On Mother's Day, in the year 2000, the Million Mom March was held in Washington, D.C. This demonstration was designed to make government representatives and other citizens aware of the lives that have been harmed or destroyed by guns and of the need for gun control.

Which of the following is the characteristic of democracy that is shown by the Million Mom March?

○ A. The people have religious freedom.
○ B. A person has the right to a trial by jury in a noncriminal case involving more than $20.
○ C. The people cannot be forced to house and feed soldiers in their homes.
○ D. All people have the right of free speech and the right to gather peacefully.

41. In 1962, Ne Win, a general in the Burmese army in Burma, used force to take over control of his country. In 1990, his government changed the name of the country to Myanmar, although many do not recognize the right of the military government to change the name. The leader remains in power through fear, murders, forced labor, arrests, and torture.

Burma is an example of which of the following forms of government?

○ A. monarchy
○ B. democracy
○ C. dictatorship
○ D. leadership

42. In Saudi Arabia, the king has both executive and legislative power. Most positions of power are held by relatives of the king. Although there are no political parties, citizens submit requests for help or complaints to the king.

Monarchal, democratic, or dictatorial types of governments have different characteristics.

Based upon the reading selection, Saudi Arabia has what type of government?

_____

43. In the city of Monroe Falls, Ohio, the railroad tracks run through the center of town, crossing State Route 91. Traffic on Route 91 becomes backed-up every time a train passes through the city. This creates a problem for the residents on the north side of the tracks, because they are cut off from the fire station and emergency personnel, which are located south of the tracks. Emergency personnel have to go through the neighboring towns of Cuyahoga Falls or Kent to get to the north side. As a result, the city is studying the possibility of building a second fire station on the north side of the railroad tracks.

What is the main idea of the reading selection?

_____

_____

_____

44. Citizens living along the Cuyahoga River in northeastern Ohio were disturbed by the quality of the river. The water was full of litter, broken limbs, branches, and dead animals. When the citizens decided to clean up the river, they declared one Saturday in May "River Day." Girl Scout and Boy Scout troops, members of various churches and garden clubs, and classes from the local high school picked up trash and debris. Some volunteers wore boots and waded in the water to clean up areas that could not be reached otherwise. Local merchants provided free lunches for the volunteers. After the work was finished, the volunteers had the satisfaction of knowing the river not only looked more beautiful, it was cleaner and healthier, too.

Which of the following is the main idea of the reading selection?

○ A. Local merchants provided free lunches for the volunteers.
○ B. The water was full of litter, broken limbs, branches, and dead animals.
○ C. Citizens living along the Cuyahoga River, disturbed about the water quality, worked to clean the river.
○ D. Some volunteers wore boots and waded into the water.

45. Some of the citizens of Hudson, Ohio, are upset about plans to build 70 town houses on Prospect Street. The citizens feel the town houses will change the character of the neighborhood. They are also concerned the town houses will increase the population density of the neighborhood. The citizen group hired an attorney and filed a request with City Council to have the building of town houses removed from the city's list of acceptable land uses.

Which of the following is the main idea of the reading selection?

○ A. Some citizens of Hudson, Ohio, are upset about plans to build 70 town houses on Prospect Street.
○ B. The town houses would change the character of the neighborhood.
○ C. The town houses would increase the population density of the neighborhood.
○ D. The citizen group hired an attorney.

46. In Oil City, Pennsylvania, citizens felt the small, triangular park beside the main intersection going into the city needed to be more attractive. As a result, one Saturday morning in May, a group of volunteers gathered at the park and planted flowers.

Name one advantage and one disadvantage of this solution to the problem.

_____

_____

_____

_____

47. Members of a bicycle club in Destin, West Virginia, wanted the city to build trails on which they could ride their bikes without having to worry about traffic.

Which of the following strategies could the bicycle club use to obtain their goal?

○ A. Collect signatures on petitions to place a levy to build bike trails on the ballot in the next election.
○ B. Pass a law forbidding cars to travel on the roads in and around Destin.
○ C. Put up road blocks across the highways leading into the town.
○ D. Make people pay a tax each time they drive their cars.

48. When their fifteen-year-old son begins to play music loudly, Mr. and Mrs. Dennison become very upset. They both dislike the music and feel they should be able to sit in their living room without having to listen to music they do not enjoy.

Which of the following would be a fair and just solution to the problem?

- ○ A. tell their son, David, he may no longer listen to any music
- ○ B. refuse to allow David to talk on the phone for one week
- ○ C. allow David to listen quietly to his music in his room
- ○ D. make David take out the trash

49. Because several new factories moved into the town of Baybridge, the population increased and two new elementary schools were needed. Members of the Board of Education decided both schools would be built on the west side of town where the wealthiest citizens lived. One member of the Board told the local newspaper this was a fair and just solution because the wealthy citizens were the ones who earned the most money and paid the most taxes.

Explain whether this is a fair and just decision, and state reasons for your response.

_____

_____

_____

_____

50. Fidel Castro, the present leader of Cuba, gained control of the country in 1959 by over-throwing Fulgencio Batista, the former dictator. Since that time, Amnesty International, an organization that reports on abuses of human rights throughout the world, has reported yearly that the Cuban government has had numerous human rights violations. The government does not allow its citizens freedom of expression, assembly, or privacy, and citizens who speak out against the government have been given long prison terms, harassed, or exiled.

Use the selection above to determine which of the statements most accurately describes the role of the citizens in the Cuban government.

- ○ A. Citizens speak freely and express their opinions to help improve Cuba's government.
- ○ B. Citizens regularly vote for a number of candidates, and the head of state changes often as a result of these elections.
- ○ C. Citizens are not permitted to speak out against the government and have little voice in the running of the country.
- ○ D. Citizens often attend meetings to discuss the government and changes they would like to see.

51. In 1989, in the People's Republic of China, student members of a pro-democracy movement demanded the removal of top Communist government officials. On April 20, the government ordered the students to end the demonstrations. On May 4, about 100,000 students and workers met in Tiananmen Square to express their demands for removal of the government officials and more rights and freedoms for the people. The government promptly sent in the People's Liberation Army, which crushed the demonstrations. In the process, they killed hundreds of protesters, injured 10,000, and arrested hundreds of people. In order to stop the protests in favor of democracy, the government made many arrests, conducted quick trials, and executed those found guilty. The foreign press was banned from the country, and the Chinese press was strictly controlled.

Which of the following most accurately describes the way in which the people of the People's Republic of China participate in the government under the present leadership?

○ A. The people have religious freedom.
○ B. The people have all the rights and freedoms that are enjoyed by citizens of the United States.
○ C. The people are not permitted to protest the government, and freedom of the press is not allowed.
○ D. The people are not permitted to worship as they choose.

52. When Beth Danford arrived in Paris, she was immediately aware there was going to be an election. The newspapers were full of articles about the campaign, and the people were passing out flyers urging citizens to vote for the candidates of various parties. Upon asking, Beth found out the election was not only for the president, but also for some members of the parliament.

Explain how the citizens participate in the political system of France.

_____

_____

_____

_____

End of Citizenship Test 1

Citizenship

Test 2

Use the time line titled "North America and Europe from 1900 to 1920" to answer question 1.

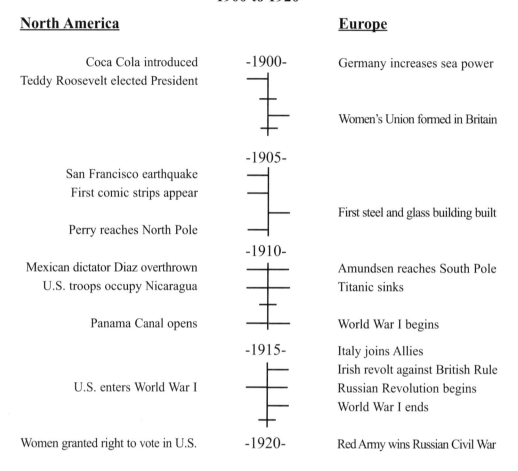

**North America and Europe from
1900 to 1920**

North America   **Europe**

Coca Cola introduced   -1900-   Germany increases sea power
Teddy Roosevelt elected President

                                                          Women's Union formed in Britain

                                          -1905-
San Francisco earthquake
First comic strips appear

                                                          First steel and glass building built
Perry reaches North Pole

                                          -1910-
Mexican dictator Diaz overthrown   Amundsen reaches South Pole
U.S. troops occupy Nicaragua   Titanic sinks

Panama Canal opens   World War I begins

                                          -1915- Italy joins Allies
                                                   Irish revolt against British Rule
U.S. enters World War I   Russian Revolution begins
                                                   World War I ends

Women granted right to vote in U.S. -1920- Red Army wins Russian Civil War

1. What occurred in Europe during the same year Coca Cola was introduced in the United States?

   _____

2. The Revolutionary War period in the history of the United States was the period of time during which the Revolutionary War was fought.

   Which of the following events occurred during the Revolutionary War period?

   ○ A. The first Thanksgiving was celebrated.
   ○ B. General George Washington led an army of Americans against the British army.
   ○ C. The Internet was developed.
   ○ D. The battle at the Alamo was fought.

3. When the patio of a winery on Middle Bass Island in Lake Erie collapsed, reporters rushed to cover the story. Among the people questioned were a mother whose son was visiting the winery, the friend of one of the waiters who worked at the winery, and one of the visitors who was injured when the patio fell.

   Of the people questioned, who is the most reliable source for relating the actual events that took place?

   Explain your answer.

   _____

4. Who would be the most reliable source for relating the events that occurred following the bombing of the Federal Building in Oklahoma City on April 19, 1995?

   ○ A. a survivor who was in the building at the time of the bombing
   ○ B. the family of one of the people who was killed in the bombing
   ○ C. the mother of one of the survivors
   ○ D. the reporter who wrote an article for the local newspaper

5. Benjamin Franklin was born in 1706 in Boston, Massachusetts. Because of his many talents and achievements, he later became the most famous person in the colonies. As a writer, he founded the first newspaper in Philadelphia and published *Poor Richard's Almanac*, a book that sold more copies than any other book except the Bible. As a scientist and an inventor, he became famous for his experiments with electricity and for his inventions including the lightning rod, bifocals, and a wood-burning stove. He started Philadelphia's first public library, its first hospital, and the world's first volunteer fire department. In 1740, Franklin founded Pennsylvania's first college, which later became the University of Pennsylvania. In government, Benjamin Franklin was a signer of the Declaration of Independence, a delegate to the Continental Congress, and a delegate to the Constitutional Convention. Because of his many contributions, Benjamin Franklin is known today as one of the greatest men in the history of the United States.

   Name two of Benjamin Franklin's achievements that affected the way in which American people live today.

   _____

   _____

6. When Montezuma II, the Emperor of the Aztec empire from 1502 to 1520, began his reign, his empire was powerful, rich, and civilized. Aztec people had a well developed government that collected taxes, provided famine relief, made laws, and provided punishment. A strong army protected the nation and conquered the nation's enemies. The art and architecture were amazingly beautiful.

In 1519, Hernan Cortes arrived in what later became Mexico. When Montezuma heard of the arrival of men with metal skin (armor) and yellow hair, he believed a god had arrived. At first, he tried to trick Cortes and his men, but then he invited them to Tenochtitlan, the capital of the Aztec empire. When Montezuma began listening to the wishes and demands of Cortes, Montezuma's noblemen and military leaders became upset and feared for the safety of the Aztec empire. Cortes and his men planned to assassinate Montezuma. Montezuma was killed in 1520. The following year, Cuauhtemoc, who followed Montezuma as emperor, surrendered to Cortes.

Which of the following caused Montezuma to lose his life and his power?

- ○ A. He had a powerful and advanced empire.
- ○ B. Montezuma believed Cortes was a god and invited him to the capital of the Aztec empire.
- ○ C. A strong army protected the nation and conquered the nation's enemies.
- ○ D. Cuauhtemoc followed Montezuma as emperor.

7. Francisco (Pancho) Villa was born into a poor family in Mexico in the year 1877. When he was a child, he realized only the very wealthy owned land, and the poor were treated like slaves. When he was fifteen years old, Villa shot a man who was attempting to harm his sister. Villa fled to the mountains where he lived as a fugitive. In 1909, he joined rebel leader Francisco I. Madero in the revolution against Porfirio Diaz. By joining the revolution, Villa hoped to help improve the lives of the poor.

Which of the following caused Pancho Villa to flee to the mountains?

- ○ A. He did not like his sister.
- ○ B. He wanted to fight in the Mexican American War.
- ○ C. He shot a man.
- ○ D. He wanted to fight the dictator.

8. The Society of Friends, commonly called Quakers, believes a person does not need a spiritual guide to God. Each individual can find and understand God through an inward light supplied by the Holy Spirit. Members of this religion attend meetings that include long periods of silent meditation and prayers offered by those who are moved by the Spirit. The Quakers believe in peace, simplicity, and equality among all races and both sexes.

The Shakers were members of the United Society of Believers in Christ's Second Coming. This religion began in England under the leadership of Ann Lee. The Shakers moved to the United States in 1774, where they lived until their religion became extinct around 1980. The Shakers, so called because of their shaking during worship, believed in equality of the sexes, but not marriage or reproduction. For a short period of time, their numbers grew because of the joining of new converts and through adoption. Finally, their practice of not marrying or reproducing led to the end of the organization.

Which of the following statements is true about the Quakers and the Shakers?

- ○ A. Both believe in the of equality men and women.
- ○ B. They were both started by Ann Lee.
- ○ C. Both groups have many members today.
- ○ D. They both like to adopt many children.

9. The American colonies were considered lands of opportunity for most Europeans who came to the American shores. Europeans found religious freedom, cheap land, increased job opportunities, and a more comfortable way of life. On the other hand, the black slaves were forced to work long hours for their owners with no chance of escape to a better life. The owners enforced slave codes that forbade the slaves from practicing their own religion, marrying, owning property, or learning to read. Owners also had the right to sell a slave's family members to others. Slaves had neither freedom nor equality in their new homes.

Which of the following statements is true of life in the American colonies?

- ○ A. Both Europeans and slaves considered the American colonies to be lands of opportunity.
- ○ B. Both Europeans and slaves found religious freedom, cheap land, increased job opportunities, and a more comfortable way of life.
- ○ C. Europeans were forced to work long hours for their owners with no chance of escape to a better life.
- ○ D. Slaves were forced to work long hours for their owners with no chance of escape to a better life.

10. In the early 1500s, the Spanish established the colony of New Spain, that included Mexico, Central America, islands of the Caribbean, Florida, and parts of what is now the western United States`. Life became difficult for the Native Americans who were living in New Spain. The Spanish conquerors destroyed their books, spread diseases, refused to allow the Native Americans to practice their religions, and forced them into slavery. From 1519 to 1568, the Native American population of Mexico decreased by at least five million.

What was one of reasons the Native American population of Mexico decreased?

_____

11. In the years before the Civil War, the freed African-American population endured many hardships. After a slave revolt in 1831, terrified whites killed over 100 slaves and freed blacks. African-Americans were forbidden to gather in public places or to hold their own religious services. Slave catchers, who searched the cities looking for escaped slaves, would often capture freed African-Americans and sell them back into slavery. Other African-Americans found that the whites would not hire them for skilled jobs. They were not permitted to enter lecture halls, restaurants, or hotels. They were also denied the right to vote.

Which of the following statements can be inferred from reading the selection above?

○ A. Many freed African-Americans found jobs as skilled laborers.
○ B. Freed African-Americans were treated the same as the white citizens.
○ C. Life was difficult for freed African-Americans.
○ D. Freed African-Americans became very rich in this country.

12. Puritans, a group of English Protestants who believed the Church of England followed too many practices of the Roman Catholic Church, arrived in Massachusetts in 1630. They wanted to establish a colony that would be a model for the rest of the world to follow. In their colony, each man was required to promise that his family would follow the rules of the Puritan Church. Each person was required to help with the construction of the community. The children of all members of the community were offered a free education.

Which of the following statements is true about the contribution of the Puritans to the American culture?

○ A. They established a pattern of complete religious tolerance.
○ B. Each person worked for himself, not for the good of the community.
○ C. They followed many of the practices of the Roman Catholic Church.
○ D. They established a system of free education for all children of the community.

13. The Cajuns are French descendants who migrated from Nova Scotia, Canada, to southern Louisiana around 1755. They brought their French language, music, and cooking. Because they lived relatively isolated in the swamps and lowlands, they changed less than many of the other immigrant groups that came to this country. An estimated 500,000 Cajuns still live in southern Louisiana, where they maintain the customs and traditions of their ancestors. Today, Cajun food is served in restaurants throughout the United States, and Cajun music can be heard throughout Louisiana.

What is one of the greatest influences the Cajuns have had on the culture of the United States?

_____

Use the map titled "Map of the World" to answer question 14.

Map of the World

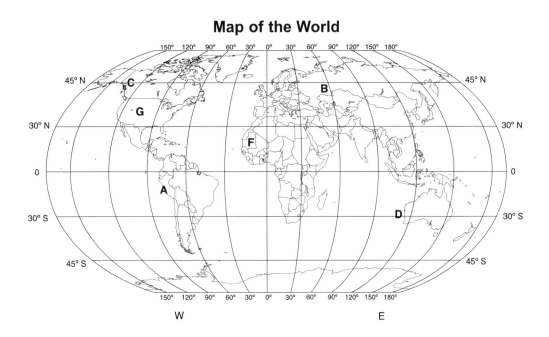

14. What are the coordinates for letter B on the map?

   ○ A. 40° N and 55° E
   ○ B. 45° N and 140° W
   ○ C. 30° S and 110° E
   ○ D. 55° N and 40° E

15. What part of a map would you need to use to find the distance from one location to another?

    ○ A. the title of the map
    ○ B. the compass rose
    ○ C. the scale
    ○ D. the key or legend

Use the map titled "Time Zones of the Continental United States" to answer questions 16 and 17.

Time Zones of the Continental United States

Eastern Standard Time
Central Standard Time
Mountain Standard Time
Pacific Standard Time

16. Christopher Bell lives in the Eastern Standard time zone. He wants to make a phone call to someone living in the Central Standard time zone.

    If it is 9:30 p.m. at Christopher's house, what time is it in the Central Standard time zone?

    ○ A. 8:30 a.m.
    ○ B. 8:30 p.m.
    ○ C. 10:30 a.m.
    ○ D. 10:30 p.m.

17. Penny Davis traveled from her home in Valpariso, Florida, which is in the Eastern Standard time zone, to the home of her brother in San Fransico, California, in the Pacific Standard time zone.

If Penny left her house at 8:00 a.m. and the trip took five hours, what time did she arrive at her brother's house?

   ○ A. 10:00 a.m.
   ○ B. 11:00 a.m.
   ○ C. noon
   ○ D. 1:00 p.m.

Use the maps titled "Nomadic Animal Herding" and "Annual Rainfall in Inches" to answer question 18.

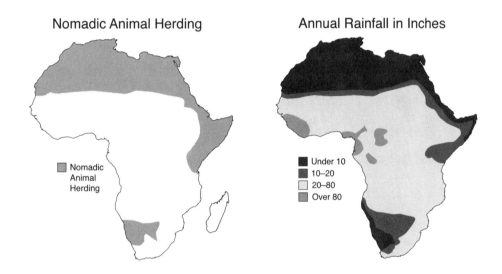

18. People living in the interior areas of Africa have different customs and ways of life than people living in the northernmost part of the continent.

After looking at the maps, "Nomadic Animal Herding" and "Annual Rainfall in Africa," explain how and why northern Africa is different from most of the rest of Africa in the way people use the land.

_____

_____

_____

Use the maps titled "Economic Activities" and "Tundra" to answer question 19.

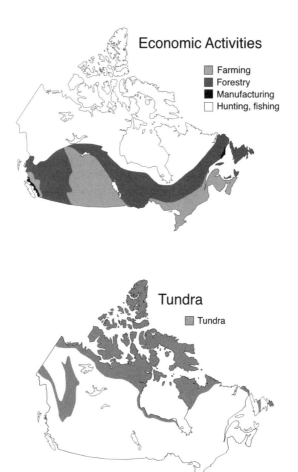

19. The map titled "Economic Activities" shows the economic activities of Canada, and the map titled "Tundra" shows the areas of Canada that are covered with tundra.

   Which of the following can be determined by studying the two maps?

   ○ A. The main economic activity in the tundra region of Canada is farming.
   ○ B. The main economic activity in the tundra region of Canada is forestry.
   ○ C. The main economic activity in the tundra region of Canada is manufacturing.
   ○ D. The main economic activities in the tundra region of Canada are hunting and fishing.

20. The president of the United States travels all over the world to meet with leaders of other nations.

    What is one reason the president travels the world?

    ○ A. The president enjoys meeting new people.
    ○ B. The president meets with leaders to establish positive political relationships.
    ○ C. The president enjoys buying goods in foreign markets for his children.
    ○ D. The president must spy on other nations to protect the people of the United States.

21. Louisa, a sixth grader from France, recently completed one year as an exchange student. She stayed with a family in Ohio and went to a middle school in a small, rural area. Louisa's home in France is located about five minutes from Paris, a major metropolis.

    Identify three things Louisa learned from her year as an exchange student in America.

    _____

22. Milk chocolate, a favorite food of many Americans, is made by combining ground kernels of cocoa beans, sugar, cocoa butter, natural and artificial flavors, and concentrated milk.

    Cocoa beans are an example of which of the following factors of production?

    ○ A. land
    ○ B. labor
    ○ C. capital
    ○ D. entrepreneurship

23. Brent decides to open a hot dog stand at the park. He buys a small cart with an umbrella to use as his stand. He hires his friend Lisa to work there. He buys hot dogs, buns, and condiments from a local vendor. Brent also rents a small area for his cart from the park's management department.

    This reading selection involves several factors of production.

    Which component of the selection refers to entrepreneurship?

    _____

24. An entrepreneur decides to open an exercise facility in a wealthy neighborhood of the city in which he lives. The research company he hired to determine whether the exercise facility should be located in that neighborhood, found that residents of the neighborhood are very interested in everything related to good health. The research company also found there are no exercise gyms or facilities in the area.

What factor influenced the entrepreneur's decision to open the exercise facility in that location?

○ A. The entrepreneur wanted to provide members of his community with jobs.
○ B. demand
○ C. supply
○ D. The entrepreneur had money he wanted to invest.

25. When Sam Edwards decided to buy a new DVD player, he read the ads in the Sunday newspaper. He found a SuperPlay brand DVD player at Buy Mart for $250.00. Shop Stop had an Ace brand DVD player for $200.00. The advertisement for the SuperPlay brand featured Sam's favorite singer. Sam bought the SuperPlay DVD player.

Which of the following factors influenced Sam's decision to purchase the SuperPlay brand DVD player?

○ A. price
○ B. advertising
○ C. quality
○ D. packaging

26. The Cleveland Cavaliers found they were playing games in an arena that had many empty seats. After several seasons, they lowered the cost of the tickets.

Explain how the law of supply and demand caused the price of the Cleveland Cavaliers tickets to change.

_____

_____

_____

_____

27. Tessa noticed, throughout the city, whenever she saw a Burger Chef, she also saw a King Burger within one block. The two burger chains were major competitors.

How does the presence of these competitors benefit the consumer?

   ○ A. When demand exceeds supply, prices drop.
   ○ B. Consumers have fewer choices if there are only two competitors.
   ○ C. When supply exceeds demand, prices rise.
   ○ D. Competition forces producers to keep prices down.

28. The United States does not produce enough petroleum to meet all the needs of the nation. Petroleum-rich countries of the Middle East do not have the factories needed to produce manufactured goods and, therefore, do not produce enough heavy machinery.

Based upon the reading selection, explain the trade relationship between some of the petroleum-rich countries of the Middle East and the United States.

_____

_____

_____

29. What is the main function of the legislative branch of government?

_____

_____

30. Which of the following is an activity carried out by the executive branch of government?

   ○ A. writing proposed legislation and holding committee hearings
   ○ B. appointing officials and coordinating work of agencies
   ○ C. conducting trials
   ○ D. sentencing convicted persons

31. John Davidson and his wife, Sarah, were upset with some of the votes their state senator cast in a recent session of the State Legislature. The Davidsons appeared on a local TV talk show to discuss their feelings. They encouraged voters to replace the senator in the next election.

The Davidson's ability to speak out publicly is known as freedom of speech.

Freedom of speech represents what characteristic of democracy?

○ A. the right to assemble
○ B. a basic right guaranteed by the Constitution
○ C. the right to practice religion
○ D. the right and responsibility to vote

32. Residents in a small town were upset because a group of people purchased a building in which to hold religious services. When reporters questioned the residents, they stated everything would be fine if the new church were a "normal" church. They did not consider the church "normal" because the members of the congregation prayed to "Mother Earth" and "Father Sky." When the residents tried to use the courts to remove the church, they were told the members of the congregation had the right to worship in that church.

Which characteristic of democracy is shown in the reading selection?

○ A. People have religious freedom.
○ B. Americans are guaranteed freedom of the press.
○ C. separation of church and state
○ D. All people have the right of free speech and the right to gather peacefully.

33. On March 6, 1999, the ruler of Bahrain, Sheik Isa bin Salman Al Khalifa, died of natural causes. His oldest son, Sheik Hamad bin Isa Al Khalifa, followed his father to become the sole leader of the country. He rules with no parliament or senate, and the country does not have a constitution. When this ruler dies, he also will be replaced by his oldest son.

Bahrain is an example of which of the following forms of government?

○ A. monarchy
○ B. democracy
○ C. dictatorship
○ D. leadership

34. Below is a list of characteristics for monarchal, democratic, and dictatorial governments. Assign each of these characteristics to a specific type of government using the table below.

   • headed by a single leader (king or queen)

   • people hold the power to govern

   • titles are inherited

   • headed by one person holding total power

   • people are guaranteed the right to vote for their leaders

   • power gained through force

Monarchy	Democratic	Dictatorship

35. The Board of Zoning Appeals in Suffield Township turned down the requests of two families to begin sand and gravel mining on their farms. The Board reasoned these farms were in residential areas where the zoning code would not permit mining. Many of the eighty residents attending the meeting were neighbors of the areas in which the mining was to take place. These people stated they were concerned with the damage to the environment and the decrease in property values. Members of the families stated they needed to begin the mining operations because farming was no longer profitable for them. They also stated the lake created by the mining operation would increase property values of lands around the mines.

What is the main idea of the reading selection?

_____

_____

_____

36. Members of the West Lincoln High School marching band and members of the band boosters group are upset because the superintendent wants to forbid band travel outside the state. The band boosters group raises more than $135,000 yearly to support the band and its activities. The superintendent says the ban on out-of-state travel is the result of a decline in enrollment in the marching band.

Which of the following is the main idea of the reading selection?

○ A. People are upset the superintendent wants to forbid band travel outside the state.
○ B. The band boosters group raises more than $135,000 yearly to support the activities of the band.
○ C. People should have the right to vote for the marching band.
○ D. The ban on out-of-state travel is the result of a decline in enrollment in the marching band.

37. Recently, several technology companies have expressed interest in relocating their offices to the city of Randolph. Randolph's City Council would like to offer benefits to these companies for relocating to this city. One council member suggested offering free classes for citizens interested in learning technological skills.

Why would the council member suggest offering free technology classes?

○ A. The technology companies would pay fewer taxes.
○ B. The technology companies would know members of the city council.
○ C. The technology companies would have a larger number of potential employees.
○ D. Randolph's citizens would accept lower wages.

38. Tom Brown, the manager of a local pharmacy, realized many senior citizens were having trouble finding ways to get to the doctor, the grocery store, and the pharmacy. He decided he would find a way to help these senior citizens.

Which of the following is an appropriate action to take to solve the problem?

○ A. Pass a law requiring anyone going to the doctor, the grocery store, or the pharmacy to take a senior citizen along.
○ B. Pass a law requiring all stores to provide free delivery service for all senior citizens.
○ C. Talk with other people, and begin a network of volunteers who would sign up to help senior citizens with their transportation needs.
○ D. Make people pay a tax each time they drive their cars.

39. Many citizens in the town of Jackson are upset because children who live on the east side have access to several parks and playgrounds, but similar facilities are not available on the west side.

Which of the following is a fair and just solution to the problem?

○ A. Stop all children from using any of the parks or playgrounds.
○ B. Close all parks.
○ C. Begin legislation to build a new park on the west side.
○ D. Force the parents of the children who live on the west side to take their children to the east side parks and playgrounds every day.

40. Madagascar is a country located off the east coast of Africa. Its constitution states that a president, who is elected by the people, serves a seven-year term. Members of the National People's Assembly, which is similar to our Senate, are elected by the citizens for five-year terms.

Use the selection above to determine which of the statements most accurately describes the role of the citizens in the government of Madagascar.

○ A. The citizens are not able to speak freely and express their opinions.
○ B. The citizens are not permitted to vote for candidates to represent them in government.
○ C. The citizens are permitted to vote for the president and for representatives to the National People's Assembly.
○ D. The citizens are not permitted to worship in the churches of their choice.

End of Citizenship Test 2

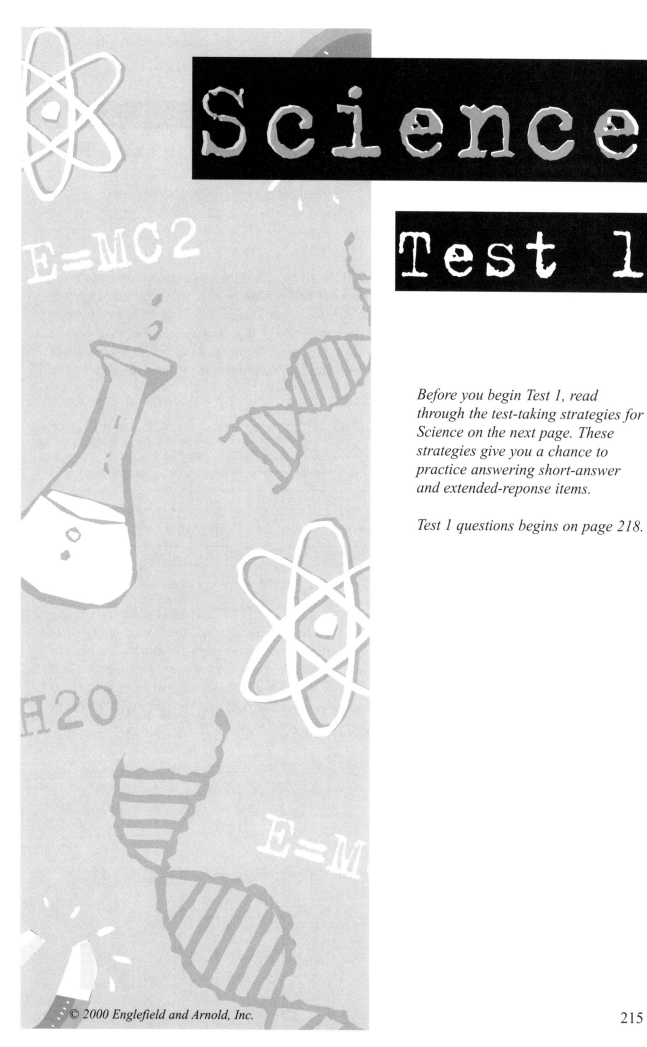

Science

Test 1

Before you begin Test 1, read through the test-taking strategies for Science on the next page. These strategies give you a chance to practice answering short-answer and extended-reponse items.

Test 1 questions begins on page 218.

Short-Answer Items

Read through the question below.

Antibiotics are medications that have saved the lives of millions of children and adults all over the world. Since antibiotics were invented half a century ago, there have been fewer deaths from illnesses caused by bacteria. This has prolonged the lives of many people. Unfortunately, antibiotics are becoming less effective in fighting disease because certain bacteria are now immune to the effects of antibiotics. Scientists have found that because antibiotics have been used so often, certain bacteria have developed defenses against the medication.

What are two ways in which scientists and doctors can keep antibiotics effective in fighting disease?

_____
_____
_____
_____
_____
_____

The following is an example of a 2-point response:

There are many ways in which scientists and doctors could keep antibiotics effective in fighting disease. Maybe doctors should only treat very sick people with antibiotics instead of using antibiotics for every person with a cold. Scientists could prevent sickness through cleaner water and safer food. They could fortify more food with vitamins so immune systems would be stronger and could fight illnesses more effectively. Scientists may even be able to develop new antibiotics that the bacteria have not developed defenses against.

Extended-Response Items

Read through the question below.

Amber lives in a town called Sunnyville where the population is growing very quickly. Everyone wants to move to Sunnyville. There are many jobs coming to Sunnyville. In fact, two large factories that make tires and paint were built. Sunnyville is not located in a desert, but the area around Sunnyville is dry and usually hot. The Crystal River runs through Sunnyville and provides most of Sunnyville's water supply.

Given what you know about Sunnyville, what inferences can you make about pollution in Sunnyville both now and in the future?

_____
_____
_____
_____
_____
_____
_____
_____
_____

The following is an example of a 4-point response:

The pollution in Sunnyville will probably increase as the population increases. Having more people and more factories in Sunnyville will increase automobile pollution from extra cars, sewage from new homes that are being built, and water pollution from the factories. Also, more garbage will be generated because of the increase in population in Sunnyville. There will be noise pollution from the extra people and the factories, and there will be less fresh air because trees may be torn down to build houses. The pollution in Sunnyville will increase greatly unless the people find a way to solve these problems.

1. Maria Luisa Hidalgo's teacher gave her a clear crystal and Key A. Maria Luisa noticed she could see one of her long hairs through the crystal, but the hair looked like two hairs. Using a magnet, she discovered the crystal was not magnetic. She also noticed the crystal was not the shape of a hexagon.

Using Key A, what did Maria Luisa find out about the crystal?

Key A

1. If the crystal is clear, go to number 2.
2. If the crystal has a hexagonal shape, go to number 5.   If it does not have a hexagonal shape, go to number 3.
3. If the crystal is magnetic, go to number 6.   If the crystal is not magnetic, go to number 4.
4. If the crystal produces double images of items seen through it, go to number 7.
5. This crystal is quartz.
6. This crystal is magnetite.
7. This crystal is calcite.

- ○ A. The crystal is quartz.
- ○ B. The crystal is magnetite.
- ○ C. The crystal is calcite.
- ○ D. The crystal is lead.

Use the key titled "Bear Characteristics" to answer question 2.

Bear Characteristics

1. If the bear has a heavy body, short tail, and rounded ears, go to number 2.
2. If the bear is a white carnivore with a small head and a large neck, go to number 3. If the bear is primarily a vegetarian with a large head, go to number 4.
3. This bear is a polar bear.
4. If the bear's paws are adapted for digging, go to number 5. If the bear's paws are adapted for climbing trees, go to number 6.
5. This bear is a brown bear.
6. If the bear hibernates and lives in North America, go to number 7. If the bear does not hibernate and lives in South America, go to number 8.
7. This bear is an American black bear.
8. This bear is a spectacled bear.

2. Which of the following is true regarding the American black bear?

    ○ A. The bear does not hibernate, and it lives in South America.
    ○ B. The bear's paws are adapted for climbing trees.
    ○ C. The bear is a white carnivore with a small head and a large neck.
    ○ D. The bear's paws are adapted for digging.

Use Key B to answer question 3.

Key B

1. If the organism has no backbone, go to number 4.
2. If the organism has a backbone, go to number 3.
3. If the organism has fur and feeds its babies on mother's milk, go to number 5. If the organism has dry, scaly skin and lays tough-shelled eggs, go to number 6. If the organism has moist, scaleless skin and lays jelly-covered eggs, go to number 7.
4. This organism is an invertebrate.
5. This organism belongs to the group of animals called mammals.
6. This organism belongs to the group of animals called reptiles.
7. This organism belongs to the group of animals called amphibians.

3. Identify the characteristics of reptiles.

_____

_____

4. Students in Mr. Collon's sixth grade science class are excited to study electricity. Mr. Collon is having students conduct scientific investigations related to their study of electricity.

    Explain some safety rules students should follow as they conduct their investigations.

_____

_____

5. While working on scientific investigations involving chemicals, why should scientists try to avoid releasing toxic chemicals into the environment?

_____

_____

6. While doing investigations involving chemicals, students and scientists should always wear safety goggles.

   Which of the following is a possible outcome of not wearing goggles?

   ○ A. Your goggles could become steamed up, limiting your sight.
   ○ B. You would not be able to see the chemicals because they would look too small.
   ○ C. The environment would be damaged.
   ○ D. Chemicals could splash into your eyes, causing damage to the eyes.

7. Mrs. Davis had her class conduct a scientific investigation in which students connected an insulated wire to the top and bottom of a "AA" battery. Students could feel the wire become warm. They then made a circuit in which the "AA" battery was connected to a light bulb using two wires. Students observed the bulb light.

   From this investigation, which of the following could the students infer?

   ○ A. This is a parallel circuit.
   ○ B. The battery is producing energy because of a physical change.
   ○ C. The switch is turned off.
   ○ D. The energy stored in the battery changes from chemical energy to heat and light energy.

8. While studying plants, students in Mr. Will's sixth grade class placed radish seeds on blotting paper in a small dish. They watered the seeds as needed and observed them for several days. Students saw small roots appear, followed by stems. Using a hand lens, students could see root hairs protruding from the roots.

   Mr. Will instructed students to add a small amount of blue food coloring to the blotting paper. After 10 minutes, students again examined the seeds. They saw the root hairs had turned blue.

   What could students infer about this experiment?

   _____

   _____

   _____

   _____

9. While studying motion, Mrs. Ferrell's class covered half of a wooden board with sandpaper. They then stacked a wooden block on the side of the wooden board that was not covered. After attaching a rubber band to pull the block across the board, they measured the length of the rubber band as the block was pulled. Next, students placed a block on the side of the wooden board covered with sandpaper. The students attached a rubber band to pull the block and measured the length of the rubber band. They discovered the rubber band stretched farther when used to pull the block across the side with sandpaper.

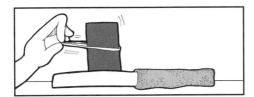 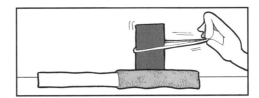

Which of the following statements could the students infer from this investigation?

○ A. The sandpaper increased the amount of friction, thus more force was necessary to move the block.
○ B. The sandpaper was expensive.
○ C. Work is the transfer of energy through both force and motion.
○ D. It would take the same amount of time for the students to pull the block of wood over any surface.

10. In 1960, the United States put into orbit the first satellite that could take pictures of the Earth's weather. Today, the United States has a series of satellites that gather information about the weather conditions around the world.

What is one advantage for using these satellites to gather weather-related information?

_____

_____

11. Although people living around airports complain, air travel has become popular as a fast, convenient means of transportation.

What is one disadvantage of increased airplane travel?

_____

12. As technology advances, Americans are using more and more electricity. Many people predict the demand on our power plants will soon exceed the capacities of the power plants. If this occurs, there will be massive blackouts. Today, the technology exists to use the power of the tides to generate electricity. In France, the world's first tidal power plant was opened in the 1960s. Canada is building a tidal power plant that will provide electricity to both Canada and the United States.

Which of the following is an advantage of building tidal power plants?

○ A. The tidal power plants could possibly cause ecological damage.
○ B. Private developers might be hurt by the government's involvement in the building of the plants.
○ C. There would be decreased demand on the use of fossil fuels to produce electricity, thus conserving those resources.
○ D. The cost of building the tidal power plants would be enormous.

Use Table 1: Major Galaxies Near Earth to answer question 13.

Table 1: Major Galaxies Near Earth

Galaxy	Shape	Distance from Milky Way (light years)
Andromeda	Spiral	2,200,000
Galaxy in Triangulum	Spiral	2,400,000
Large Magellanic Cloud	Irregular	170,000
NGC 147	Elliptical	2,200,000
NGC 185	Elliptical	2,200,000
NGC 205	Elliptical	2,200,000
NGC 221	Elliptical	2,200,000
Small Magellanic Cloud	Irregular	190,000

13. Which of the following conclusions is correct about the major galaxies near Earth?

○ A. The largest galaxy is the Large Magellanic Cloud.
○ B. The Andromeda galaxy is closest to the Milky Way.
○ C. NGC 205 has an irregular shape.
○ D. Most of the galaxies are of the elliptical shape.

Use Table 2: Climate Proportions to answer question 14.

Table 2: Climate Proportions

Climate	Continents	Oceans	Total Earth
Polar	17.0%	19.5%	18.8%
Taiga	21.3%	1.7%	7.3%
Moist temperate	15.5%	31.9%	27.2%
Moist tropical	19.9%	42.7%	36.1%
Dry	26.3%	4.2%	10.6%

14. Sally Edmonds read the "Climate Proportions" table and arrived at the following conclusions: The largest percentage of Earth has a dry climate. The smallest percentage of Earth has a polar climate.

   Evaluate Sally's conclusions, and explain how you arrived at your answer.

   _____

   _____

   _____

   _____

Use the graph titled "Percentage of Earth's Surface Covered by Rain Forests" to answer question 15.

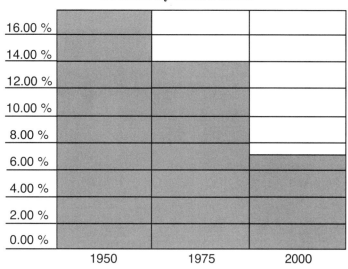

**Percentage of Earth's Surface
Covered by Rain Forests**

15. Which of the following conclusions can be made from the graph?

○ A. The rain forests of the world may disappear unless their destruction is stopped.
○ B. The rain forests of the world are quickly being replanted.
○ C. The rain forests are providing us with beautiful wood for furniture.
○ D. The rain forests that are being destroyed are in South America.

Use the illustration of Joe Warner moving a piano onto his truck to answer question 16.

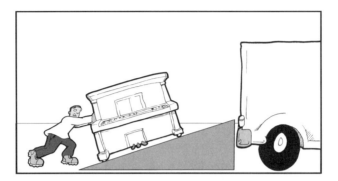

16. Which of the following is a true statement about what is occurring as Joe Warner uses the ramp to move the piano onto his truck?

   ○ A. The ramp is a simple machine that reduces work.
   ○ B. The ramp is a complex machine that is difficult to use.
   ○ C. The ramp is not a machine.
   ○ D. The ramp is a simple machine that reduces the effort for the person using it.

17. A farmer decided to store his hay on the second floor of his barn. He purchased pulleys to lift the bales of hay up to the second floor. He found that, while using one pulley, he became very tired. He added a second pulley, which reduced the amount of effort he needed to use to lift the bales of hay up to the second floor of the barn.

   Explain why less effort was needed when the farmer added a second pulley.

   _____

   _____

   _____

   _____

18. Many scientists believe that, as the Egyptians were constructing the pyramids, they built ramps to move the huge stones into place.

   What is one disadvantage Egyptians may have faced when using ramps?

   _____

19. The Goodyear Blimp was flying north from its home base in Suffield, Ohio, to Jacob's Field, the Cleveland Indians' stadium in Cleveland, Ohio. Suddenly a strong wind began blowing from the south.

What effect will this wind have on the direction the blimp is flying?

_____

20. When a car suddenly pulled out in front of Anwar Smiley's car, he swerved to avoid a collision. Anwar's car went off the road and hit a pole at the edge of the road. Although his car stopped, Anwar was thrown forward against the seat belt. Fortunately, the seat belt prevented him from being thrown into the steering wheel or the dashboard of the car, which could have caused severe injuries.

Which of the following explains why Anwar was thrown forward when his car stopped?

○ A. Anwar's body was traveling at a constant speed, until his car hit the pole. Although the car stopped, his body stayed at that constant speed.
○ B. The driver of the other car needed to talk with Anwar.
○ C. Anwar was driving too fast.
○ D. Anwar's car was poorly designed, causing him to be thrown forward when his car hit the pole.

21. As Lauren Yerkey rowed her boat across the lake near her home, she began to think about the movement of the oars and the boat. She realized the oars were moving in one direction, and the boat was moving in the opposite direction.

Explain why the oars and the boat were moving in opposite directions.

_____

_____

22. Examples of both physical and chemical changes occur throughout our daily lives.

Which of the following is an example of a physical change?

○ A. a nail rusting
○ B. glass breaking
○ C. food spoiling
○ D. leaves burning

23. Does a physical or a chemical change take place when an egg is fried?

    Explain how you arrived at your answer.

    _____

    _____

24. Making salt water is an example of a physical change.

    State another physical change, involving water, that can occur in nature.

    _____

    _____

25. An important concept related to the study of energy is that one type of energy can be
    changed to another.

    Photosynthesis is an example of which of the following energy changes?

    ○ A. chemical energy changing to solar energy
    ○ B. light energy changing to chemical energy
    ○ C. electrical energy changing to heat energy
    ○ D. sound energy changing to electrical energy

26. The chemical energy of a burning candle converts to what two kinds of energy?

    _____

27. A windmill used to produce electricity is an example of which of the following
    energy conversions?

    ○ A. chemical energy changing to solar energy
    ○ B. light energy changing to chemical energy
    ○ C. electrical energy changing to mechanical energy
    ○ D. mechanical energy changing to electrical energy

28. While on vacation in Arizona, Rick and Chris Franklin saw water on the roadway. As they approached the water, they realized they had seen a mirage. A mirage happens when the air next to the ground is warmer than the air above it.

Which of the following explains the appearance of the mirage?

- ○ A. refraction
- ○ B. reflection
- ○ C. Doppler effect
- ○ D. evaporation

Use the illustration of the lawn mower to answer question 29.

29. Josephina Rivera, who just finished cleaning the house, is sitting on her chair. Josephina's son is mowing the lawn.

Josephina sits in her chair and listens to the lawn mower. Will the pitch of the lawn mower be higher when the lawn mower is at point A or point B?

Explain how you arrived at your answer.

_____

_____

_____

_____

30. People living near Cleveland Hopkins International Airport often report their windows rattle when airplanes pass overhead.

    Explain what causes the windows to rattle.

    _____

    _____

31. If Earth's axis were straight up and down, how would the amount of sunlight at the North Pole compare to the amount of sunlight at the South Pole during the summer?

    _____

    _____

32. Which of the following statements is true about the relationship between the seasons and Earth's orbit around the sun?

    ○ A. Earth's orbit, which has an elliptical shape, has a strong effect on the seasons.
    ○ B. The Northern Hemisphere of Earth is farthest from the sun during the winter.
    ○ C. The seasons are caused by the rotation of Earth.
    ○ D. The Northern Hemisphere of Earth is closest to the sun during the winter.

33. Which of the following affects the tides on the Earth's surface?

    ○ A. the time zones
    ○ B. the moon
    ○ C. daylight savings time
    ○ D. tidal waves

34. Cassandra Brown visited Carlsbad Caverns in Carlsbad, New Mexico, during her vacation. The thousands of stalactites she saw throughout the cave fascinated her. She thought they looked like giant icicles.

Which of the following best explains how stalactites are formed?

- A. Stalactites are formed by rocks being melted deep within the earth. The great pressure causes stalactites to form.
- B. Tremendous pressure pushes on the rocks and forces them to form a stalactite.
- C. Stalactites are formed by underground water dissolving the limestone. As the water evaporates, calcite is deposited on the ceiling of the cave. This calcite builds up until the stalactite is formed.
- D. A stalactite is formed by extremely high temperatures melting rock deep inside the cave.

35. Metamorphic rock, such as marble, is usually harder than sedimentary rock. Therefore, a statue made of marble would last much longer than one made of sandstone, a sedimentary rock.

Explain how metamorphic rock is formed.

_____

_____

_____

36. Archeologists were studying the ruins of a newly discovered city hidden in the jungles of Peru. One inch below the surface of the ground, they found an old knife. Two inches below the knife, they discovered a gold bracelet in the shape of what they believed to be one of the gods worshiped by the inhabitants of the ancient city. Another inch below the necklace, they found pieces of a broken clay bowl.

Based upon this information, which of the following statements is most likely true?

- A. The oldest item is the knife.
- B. The oldest item is the necklace.
- C. The oldest item is the clay bowl.
- D. All of the items are the same age.

37. Oxygen, as well as water and nitrogen, is in a constant cycle.

    Which of the following is not a true statement about the oxygen cycle?

    ○ A. Plants take in oxygen and give off carbon dioxide.
    ○ B. Organisms sometimes do not decay when they die. After thousands of years, organisms may turn into fossil fuels which are mined and burned, thus releasing carbon dioxide.
    ○ C. Animals take in oxygen and give off carbon dioxide.
    ○ D. Plants take in carbon dioxide and give off oxygen.

38. Plants are important in the cycling of resources on Earth, and they play a part in the carbon, nitrogen, and water cycles.

    Explain the role plants play in the nitrogen cycle.

    _____

    _____

    _____

    _____

39. Which of the following is a true statement about the water cycle?

    ○ A. The amount of precipitation is equal throughout the world.
    ○ B. Evaporation and condensation are parts of the water cycle.
    ○ C. Refraction is the process in which a plant releases moisture.
    ○ D. Reflection is the process in which water bounces off of the surface of the ocean.

40. Describe a food chain, and explain its relationship to a food web.

    _____

    _____

    _____

41. Each answer choice lists items along the food chain.

    Which of the following starts at the lowest level of the food chain and moves up, along the chain?

    ○ A. rabbit, flower, snake, hawk
    ○ B. snake, rabbit, flower, hawk
    ○ C. flower, rabbit, snake, hawk
    ○ D. hawk, flower, snake, rabbit

42. What type of organism gets its food by breaking down dead organisms into nutrients?

    _____

43. Different adaptations help organisms meet their needs. As a result of such adaptations, some plants have thorns.

    Which of the following is the reason for plants adapting thorns?

    ○ A. The thorns allow the plant to get the most sunlight to make the most sugar.
    ○ B. The thorns keep the plant warmer and protect it against the cold night air.
    ○ C. The thorns keep animals away that might eat the plant.
    ○ D. The thorns allow the plant to sway in the breeze.

44. Migration is a behavior adaptation seen frequently in nature. Millions of Monarch butterflies migrate from parts of the United States and Canada to Mexico for the winter.

    Why do Monarch butterflies migrate?

    _____

    _____

    _____

    _____

Use the illustration of the talon to answer question 45.

45. Eagles, falcons, and hawks have sharp, curved talons.

    Which of the following is the reason for the structure of eagles', falcons', and hawks' talons?

    ○ A. to help them to catch fish with their beaks
    ○ B. to allow them to eat seeds more easily
    ○ C. to allow them to catch and eat other animals
    ○ D. to help them to swim more easily

46. A healthy diet includes a combination of carbohydrates, fruits, vegetables, dairy products, meats, and fats.

    If someone decided only to eat fruit, how would this affect his or her diet?

    Explain your answer.

    _____

    _____

    _____

47. In planning and developing an exercise program, which of the following statements are true and should be followed?

    ○ A. Make sure you plan to increase the duration of the program gradually.
    ○ B. Include only exercises that increase your strength.
    ○ C. In weight training, increase the weight each day.
    ○ D. Start the program with as much exercise as you intend to do throughout the program.

48. Which of the following is not appropriate first aid for a burn?

    ○ A. Keep the burn cool with clean water.
    ○ B. Cover the burn with a clean dressing that will not stick to the burn.
    ○ C. If the burn is severe, call 911.
    ○ D. Apply butter to the burn.

49. Over the past several decades, large amounts of chemicals have been dumped or washed into the ocean from factories and hospitals.

What is one impact of the presence of these chemicals in ocean water?

_____

_____

_____

_____

50. The Willamette Forest of Oregon is an area where huge trees, that are hundreds of years old, grow. Environmentalists and loggers, who live in and around this ancient forest, cannot agree on whether these old-growth trees should be cut down.

Give one argument the environmentalists might use in favor of not cutting down these ancient trees. Then give one argument the loggers might use in favor of cutting down these ancient trees.

_____

_____

_____

_____

51. Plants and animals can be harmed by the actions of humans.

Which of the following is not a possible outcome of the destruction of the rain forests around the world?

○   A. There will be more medicines discovered because of the trees that are cut down.
○   B. There will be increased global warming.
○   C. Plant and animal species will disappear.
○   D. There would be a disruption of the carbon dioxide and oxygen levels in the atmosphere.

End of Science Test 1

Science

Test 2

Use the key titled "Bear Characteristics" to answer question 1.

Bear Characteristics

1. If the bear has a heavy body, short tail, and rounded ears, go to number 2.
2. If the bear is a white carnivore with a small head and a large neck, go to number 3. If the bear is primarily a vegetarian with a large head, go to number 4.
3. This bear is a polar bear.
4. If the bear's paws are adapted for digging, go to number 5. If the bear's paws are adapted for climbing trees, go to number 6.
5. This bear is a brown bear.
6. If the bear hibernates and lives in North America, go to number 7. If the bear does not hibernate and lives in South America, go to number 8.
7. This bear is an American black bear.
8. This bear is a spectacled bear.

1. Dominique visited the zoo and saw a white bear with a small head.

   What type of bear did she see?

   ○ A. an American black bear
   ○ B. a polar bear
   ○ C. a spectacled bear
   ○ D. a brown bear

Use Key B to answer question 2.

Key B

1. If the organism has no backbone, go to number 4.
2. If the organism has a backbone, go to number 3.
3. If the organism has fur and feeds its babies on mother's milk, go to number 5. If the organism has dry, scaly skin and lays tough-shelled eggs, go to number 6. If the organism has moist, scaleless skin and lays jelly-covered eggs, go to number 7.
4. This organism is an invertebrate.
5. This organism belongs to the group of animals called mammals.
6. This organism belongs to the group of animals called reptiles.
7. This organism belongs to the group of animals called amphibians.

2. Identify the characteristics of mammals.

_____

_____

3. Students in Mr. Byron's sixth grade science class are excited about a scientific investigation they will conduct in class. Before the investigation, Mr. Byron will give a test on safety rules for using chemicals.

Which of the following is not a rule that relates to the safe use of chemicals?

○ A. Wear safety goggles when working with chemicals.
○ B. Do not taste the chemicals.
○ C. Make sure the chemicals are heated before using them.
○ D. Do not mix chemicals unless instructed to do so by the teacher.

4. Mr. Rose announced on Monday that his sixth grade class at Brownfield School was going to begin a unit on electricity. Eric was excited about the investigations his class was going to do. He arrived home that evening before his parents, so he decided to try some things with electricity. He wanted to be ahead of all the other students so he would get a good grade.

   What safety rule did Eric break?

   _____

   _____

5. While doing investigations involving animals, students and scientists should always wear gloves.

   What is a possible outcome of not wearing gloves?

   _____

   _____

6. By looking at the shape of a bird's beak, which of the following can a person infer?

   ○   A. The bird has been exposed to pollution.
   ○   B. the type of diet the bird eats
   ○   C. The bird lives in the city.
   ○   D. the number of babies the bird has

7. Throughout the world, scientists have noticed there is an increasing number of frogs with deformed bodies. These deformities include missing body parts or extra body parts.

   Which of the following can the scientists infer from these observations?

   ○   A. The world environment is changing in some way that is causing the changes in the frogs.
   ○   B. The frogs are eating more, causing them to grow more body parts.
   ○   C. The frogs are eating less, causing them to lose body parts.
   ○   D. People are at war with the frogs of the world and are giving them shots of dangerous drugs.

8. In the summer of the year 2000, scientists working in a rain forest in Africa discovered a new species of monkey. Unfortunately, the monkey was dead when they found it. The scientists found no wounds on the body, but they discovered that the skin of the monkey appeared to have a rash and patches of missing fur.

   Which of the following statements could scientists infer from this investigation?

   ○ A. The monkey died from a disease.
   ○ B. The monkey fell out of a tree.
   ○ C. Hunters killed the monkey.
   ○ D. The monkey was asleep.

9. Today, computers are found in schools, homes, and businesses. They are used for thousands of different purposes, from sending e-mail to analyzing the movements of Olympic athletes. Yet, there have been negative effects resulting from the use of computers.

   State one negative effect resulting from the use of computers.

   _____

10. Robots have gained more popularity in the manufacturing of various goods during recent years. Some doctors have even used robots to perform surgery. Many people believe this trend of using robots will continue.

    Which of the following could be an advantage of using robots to perform surgery?

    ○ A. The cost would be too high.
    ○ B. Doctors will not understand how to use the robots.
    ○ C. People in remote areas, such as on ships at sea, could have surgery through the use of a robot directed by a doctor hundreds of miles away.
    ○ D. The robot might not work because of a power outage.

11. For many years, people washed their clothes by hand and hung laundry out to dry. Today, many American families have gas or electric clothes dryers.

    What is one advantage of using a clothes dryer? What is one disadvantage of using a clothes dryer?

    _____

    _____

Use Table 1: Mass of Limestone to answer question 12.

Table 1: Mass of Limestone

Galaxy	Week 1	Week 3	Week 5	Week 7	Week 9	Week 11	Week 13
Rainwater	93	92	91	90	89	87	85
Sulfuric acid solution	86	81	78	73	69	63	43
Distilled water	89	89	89	89	89	89	89

12. Students in Mr. Shearer's science class were interested in the effect of acid rain on the limestone ledges in a nearby state park. They took samples of limestone and placed them in bowls. Each bowl was filled with either rainwater, sulfuric acid solution, or distilled water. The students compiled their findings in Table 1.

Based on the data students collected, which of the following conclusions is correct about the investigation?

○ A. The largest limestone sample was the one placed in the sulfuric acid solution.
○ B. The limestone placed in the rainwater dissolved the fastest.
○ C. The limestone placed in the sulfuric acid solution dissolved the fastest.
○ D. The limestone placed in the distilled water dissolved the fastest.

13. Juan uses a pulley to remove an engine from an old car.

Which of the following is a true statement about what is occurring as he uses the pulley to remove the engine?

○ A. The pulley is a simple machine that reduces work.
○ B. The pulley is a complex machine that is difficult to use.
○ C. The pulley is not a machine.
○ D. The pulley is a simple machine that reduces the effort needed for the person using it.

Use Table 2: Deaths Caused by People Running Red Lights from 1992 to 1998 to answer question 14.

Table 2: Deaths Caused by People Running Red Lights from 1992 to 1998

City	Population	Deaths	Rate per 100,000
Memphis, TN	614,067	49	8.0
Phoenix, AZ	1,125,599	122	10.8
Mesa, AZ	445,840	34	7.6
St. Petersburg, FL	237,480	18	7.6
Birmingham, AL	256,386	18	7.6
Dallas, TX	1,047,816	73	7.0
Albuquerque, NM	412,625	28	6.8
Louisville, KY	260,572	17	6.5
Detroit, MI	998,523	65	6.5
Tucson, AZ	333,756	26	7.8

14. Which of the following statements cannot be a conclusion based upon the information in Table 2?

    ○ A. More people were killed as a result of drivers running red lights in Phoenix than any other city.

    ○ B. The number of people per 100,000 killed as a result of drivers running red lights was the same in St. Petersburg and Birmingham.

    ○ C. Of all the cities listed, Mesa, Arizona, had the fewest number of people killed as a result of drivers running red lights.

    ○ D. Dallas, Texas, had the second largest number of people killed as a result of drivers running red lights.

15. Chris Michael had difficulty lifting the side of a heavy box with a lever and fulcrum.

How could he adjust the lever and fulcrum to reduce the amount of effort needed to lift the box?

_____

_____

16. Kid Kangaroo, the world champion four-wheeler jumper, found out early in his life that when his four-wheeler lands and slows at the end of a jump, his head moves downward toward the handlebars of the racer.

Which of the following causes this?

○ A. The four-wheeler moves too slowly.
○ B. The upper part of his body is heavy which causes it to move downward.
○ C. An object will remain at rest or in uniform motion unless acted upon by an outside force.
○ D. Kid Kangaroo wants to see how far his head will go down without it hitting the handlebars.

17. Sherry and Michelle were playing croquet in Sherry's backyard. On Sherry's turn, she hit her red ball into Michelle's green ball.

Which of the following tells what probably happened after the two balls hit each other?

○ A. The red ball began to move more slowly, and the green ball began to roll.
○ B. The red ball began to move faster, and the green ball began to roll.
○ C. The red ball began to move faster, and the green ball did not move at all.
○ D. There was no change.

18. Examples of both physical and chemical changes occur throughout our daily lives.

Which of the following is an example of a physical change?

○ A. a rusting car
○ B. a piece of paper being cut
○ C. mixing ingredients to make a cake
○ D. leaves changing colors in the Fall

19. A match burning is an example of what kind of change? Why?

_____

_____

20. Cassie found a spring in her garage. She put the spring on the floor and tightly pushed together the coils of the spring.

When Cassie took her hand off the tightened spring, the potential energy stored in the coils was transformed into what type of energy?

_____

21. An electric stove is an example of which of the following energy conversions?

   ○ A. chemical energy changing to solar energy
   ○ B. light energy changing to chemical energy
   ○ C. electrical energy changing to heat energy
   ○ D. mechanical energy changing to electrical energy

22. Which of the following is not an example of energy conservation?

   ○ A. turning off lights during the day
   ○ B. riding a bicycle rather than driving a car
   ○ C. cutting down trees so hikers will have a clear path on which to travel
   ○ D. using brown paper lunch bags several times before throwing them away

23. During a storm, you often see lightning before you hear thunder. This occurs because light waves travel faster than sound waves.

Based on this information, which of the following is true?

   ○ A. Thunder is louder during the day than in the evening.
   ○ B. When a picture is taken, you see a camera's flash before you hear the shutter move.
   ○ C. When a picture is taken, you hear a camera's shutter move before you see the flash.
   ○ D. Thunder is louder in the evening than during the day.

24. What causes the Earth's seasons?

　　　○ A. the Earth's distance from the sun
　　　○ B. changes in the Earth's temperature
　　　○ C. the alignment of planets with respect to the Earth
　　　○ D. the Earth's tilt

Use the chart titled "Phases of the Moon" to answer question 25.

Phases of the Moon

25. Which of the following correctly identifies the phases of the moon from left to right?

　　　○ A. new moon, crescent moon, first quarter moon, gibbous moon, full moon
　　　○ B. new moon, gibbous moon, last quarter moon, gibbous moon, new moon
　　　○ C. full moon, crescent moon, first quarter moon, gibbous moon, new moon
　　　○ D. new moon, second moon, half moon, third moon, full moon

26. Which of the following is a true statement?

　　　○ A. The sun revolves around the Earth.
　　　○ B. The Earth revolves around the moon.
　　　○ C. The moon revolves around the sun.
　　　○ D. The Earth revolves around the sun.

27. Combustion is a rapid chemical reaction of two or more substances resulting in the release of heat and light.

Which of the following is an example of combustion?

　　　○ A. burning coal
　　　○ B. sawing a log in half
　　　○ C. blowing up a balloon
　　　○ D. mixing together salt and water

Use the map titled "The Contour Map of the Earth's Layers" to answer question 28.

The Contour Map of the Earth's Layers

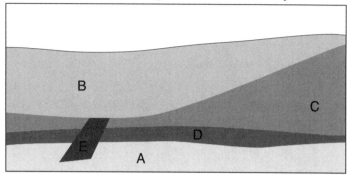

28. Which letter represents the oldest layer shown on the contour map?

   ○ A. letter E
   ○ B. letter D
   ○ C. letter A
   ○ D. letter B

29. Which of the following best explains how igneous rocks are formed?

   ○ A. Water dripping from the tops of caves causes igneous rocks to form.
   ○ B. Pressure causes igneous rocks to form.
   ○ C. Hot and cold temperatures cause igneous rocks to form.
   ○ D. Intense heat causes igneous rocks to form.

30. Tim was sitting at his desk when it began to rain. Two hours later, he looked out the window and saw the clouds had disappeared and the sun was shining, but there were puddles all over the playground. Later in the day, when Tim walked home from school, he noticed all the puddles were gone.

   Explain what happened.

   _____

   _____

31. What living thing is at the bottom of any food chain because it can produce its own food?

    ○ A. insect
    ○ B. plant
    ○ C. small animal
    ○ D. mammal

32. Different adaptations help organisms meet their needs. Some animals that live in the desert have long legs.

Which of the following is the reason for this adaptation?

    ○ A. to allow the animal to get the most sunlight to make the most sugar
    ○ B. to keep the animal warmer and protect it against the cold night air
    ○ C. to blend in with the background of the desert
    ○ D. to keep the body of the animal away from the heat of the ground

Use the diagrams of "Food Chain 1" and "Food Chain 2" to answer question 33.

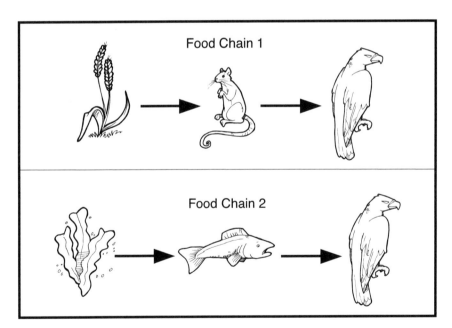

33. What do the arrows on the food chains represent?

_____

_____

34. When the temperature begins to drop in the winter, bears go into hibernation. Hibernation is a deep sleep-like state. During hibernation, bears' heart rates and body temperatures drop. Bears use stored body fat as energy to survive the long period of inactivity. They often hibernate for five to six months.

Why do bears hibernate?

○ A. The food supply is plentiful in the winter months.
○ B. Bears do not like snow.
○ C. Animals that prey on bears are more active during the winter.
○ D. The food supply is scarce during the winter months.

35. Richard Franklin's parents both have smoked cigarettes all of his life. Recently, a student at Richard's school offered him a cigarette.

Explain why Richard should not take the cigarette or begin smoking.

_____

_____

36. Scientists are finding more and more reasons why exercise should be a part of everyone's lives.

Which of the following statements is not true about the effects of exercise?

○ A. Exercise can help prevent heart disease.
○ B. Exercise can increase your strength.
○ C. Exercise can cause you to become fat.
○ D. Exercise can help you control your weight.

37. Which of the following is not a safe health practice?

○ A. Eating a well-balanced, low fat diet.
○ B. Sleeping late on the weekends to make up for not getting enough sleep during the week.
○ C. If a burn is severe, calling 911.
○ D. Making sure you get adequate exercise and sleep.

38. Beginning in the 1950s, the water in Lake Erie became so polluted, oxygen levels dropped. As a result, mayflies disappeared from the shores of the lake. In June of the year 2000, thousands of mayflies reappeared along both the north shore and the south shore of the lake.

Which of the following statements is probably true about why mayflies returned?

○ A. People have stopped much of the pollution from going into Lake Erie, and oxygen levels have improved.
○ B. The boaters on Lake Erie have stopped using mayflies for bait.
○ C. Mayflies found out Lake Erie is better than any of the other Great Lakes.
○ D. People have begun to breed mayflies so there will be some around the lake.

39. The government wants to build a new highway through a wetland area that is the habitat of an endangered frog.

Which of the following is an argument the environmentalists might use in favor of not building the highway?

○ A. None of the frogs would lose their homes.
○ B. Several smaller roads should be built instead of the highway.
○ C. It would take hundreds of years for new frogs to move back into that area.
○ D. The frogs would lose their habitat and could become extinct.

40. Two families in Suffield Township want to begin sand and gravel mining on their farms.

Which of the following is not a possible outcome of this action?

○ A. There will be more plant and animal species in the area.
○ B. There will be increased global warming.
○ C. Some plants and animals will lose their habitats.
○ D. Erosion could increase.

End of Science Test 2